MW00779149

"Christlikeness is the will of God for ev main takeaway of this book on ageing. It contains many useful thoughts for self-examination and meditation. With more time on our hands as we age, we Christians have our own visions and ideas of what we should be doing as we approach the end stage of our life. We often think about the joy of reading about the Lord and His work. Knowing more about the Lord does not make us more Christlike, though it helps. Our focus should not be about knowing more about God, but on knowing Him more. Knowing Him more through meditating Scriptures, seeking His will about whom and what to pray for, and consciously seeking to do His will 'in the levels of every day's most quiet need', will lead us to know Him more. We are encouraged to focus on deepening the relationship with Him rather than intellectual knowledge of Him."

S. Dhanabalan
Former Chairman, Temasek Holdings Ltd

"Dr. Robert Solomon has eloquently articulated the 'spiritual journey' in this remarkable book of hope. His insight, wisdom, and erudition make Growing Old Gracefully essential reading for us to reflect and contemplate. This compelling book is an inspirational guide written with scintillating clarity."

Dr. Kua Ee Heok
Tan Geok Yin Professor of Psychiatry and Neuroscience
National University of Singapore

"Distilled from Bishop Solomon's vast pastoral experience, meticulous biblical research, and review of works by well-respected theologians and Christian authors, this book is truly a treasure trove of spiritual truths, insights, and wisdom on growing old gracefully. Whilst it elucidates the vicissitudes of ageing, it also inspires hope in older adults by offering many practical tips for them to age well. The questions at the end of each chapter are very useful in stimulating deeper reflection. Although this book is written especially for those in their later years, middle-aged adults would glean many valuable insights from it too."

Dr. Helen Ko
Senior Lecturer, Graduate Gerontology Programmes,
Singapore University of Social Sciences
Executive Director, Beyond Age

"A must-read for those who are approaching or in their autumn years. Bishop Emeritus Solomon has provided a realistic view of what to expect as one grows old. His clear and reflective approach to address ageing issues from a Christian perspective, aptly supported by Scriptures, is instructive and encouraging. Growing old need not be limiting. Instead, it can liberate and help one to grow closer to Jesus, experiencing more of His joy and peace. This book will inspire readers with a renewed desire for an exciting adventure to grow old gracefully and follow Jesus to the end."

Chua Song Khim
Deputy Chief Executive, National University Health System
Elder, Bethesda Christian Centre

"I highly commend reading *Growing Old Gracefully* to anyone who desires to follow Jesus to the end! With a quintessential pastor's heart and also a medically trained physician, Bishop Revd. Dr. Solomon summarises succinctly the essential priorities to help us live and age gracefully well, based on clear biblical principles. These could well be used as a synopsis of the Christian discipleship journey from youth to old age. There is much wisdom shared and I have been edified reading it. More importantly, it is for us to practise living them!"

Dr. Peng Chung Mien
CEO, The Farrer Park Company and Farrer Park Hospital
Elder, Bethesda (Bedok-Tampines) Church

"Many books have been written on physical and psychosocial aspects of growing old, but not many have looked at it from spiritual perspectives. This book leads us on a journey of self-discovery, thinking through what may perhaps be the most challenging time in our life as we approach our twilight years. How do we cherish the moments we have? How do we relate to our family and friends? How do we remain faithful and be of service to Him till the end? Dr. Solomon provides deep insights to help us in our walk. An excellent book suitable for self or small group studies and reflection."

Dr. Pang Weng Sun
Geriatrician, National Healthcare Group

"This is an outstanding contribution to the literature on ageing well. It is beautifully organized, laced with telling illustrations, larded with incisive wisdom, fortified with relevant social research information, and written with charming elegance. This is a book that will equip you to grow old gracefully. It is suitable for group discussion as much as for personal use."

William J. Abraham
Outler Professor of Wesley Studies
Southern Methodist University, Dallas, Texas

GROWING OLD
Gracefully

Following Jesus
to the End

Robert M. Solomon

Discovery House
Publishing™

Growing Old Gracefully: Following Jesus to the End
© 2019 by Robert M. Solomon
Published by Discovery House Publishing Singapore Pte. Ltd.
All rights reserved.

Discovery House Publishing™ is affiliated with Our Daily Bread
Ministries Asia Ltd.

Requests for permission to quote from this book should be directed to:

Permissions Department
Our Daily Bread Publishing
P. O. Box 3566
Grand Rapids, MI 49501, USA

Or contact us by email at permissionsdept@odb.org.

Image used under license from Shutterstock.com
Design by Joshua Tan

ISBN 978-981-14-1836-5

In memory of my parents (Appa and Amma)
who went home to be with the Lord before
they experienced old age.

Contents

Preface

We grow old so quickly. When we are young, we maintain the illusion that we will stay young forever, with the same energy and health, and long life to look forward to. But how rapidly we travel through life, and find ourselves aged and approaching the end!

Moses observed how quickly our days on earth pass and fly away (Psalm 90:10). People are like the new grass of the morning: "In the morning it springs up new, but by evening it is dry and withered" (Psalm 90:6). Before long one becomes a "senior", an old man or old lady, and much of life has simply passed by. We are like "a mist that appears for a little while and then vanishes" (James 4:14).

How then should we view old age? How should we spend the later years of our lives? This book is written for those who are seniors—anyone 60 and above in years. By this time, you probably know that you have already passed the halfway point of life. Should this change the way we live? What should we focus on? What are our challenges, and what should we look out for?

The Bible paints two opposing views of old age. Firstly, old age is seen as a great time for undiminished faith, energy, and courage, as 85-year-old Caleb famously demonstrated, saying, "I am still as strong today as the day Moses sent me out [45 years before]" (Joshua 14:11). We read of how the righteous "will still bear fruit in old age, they will stay fresh and green" (Psalm 92:14). We also read how "Moses was a hundred and twenty years old when he died, yet his eyes were not weak nor his strength gone" (Deuteronomy 34:7) or what one of Job's friends told him, "You will come to the grave in full vigour, like sheaves gathered in season" (Job 5:26), though this was hardly comforting to the suffering Job.

Such a perspective resonates with popular phrases we hear today: "golden years", "healthy ageing", "positive ageing," "successful ageing" and the like (though some argue that these slogans have "a strong anti-ageing tendency").[1]

But the Bible also gives another view that must be taken seriously. We read about how old age brings with it deteriorating bodily functions and disabilities of many kinds, leading to loss of mobility and opportunities for social interaction. We are warned to be prepared for it, "before the days of trouble come and the years approach when you will say, 'I find no pleasure in them'" (Ecclesiastes 12:1). Paul realistically admits that "outwardly we are wasting away" (2 Corinthians 4:16), and the psalmist prays, "Do not cast me away when I am old; do not forsake me when my strength is gone" (Psalm 71:9).

In this book, we will examine both perspectives to gain a fuller and deeper perspective of old age. The book is divided into five sections covering key themes that people should think about as they age.

Section 1 explores life as a spiritual journey and how old age ("the gift of years")[2] is an important part of it. What are some of the tasks and processes we should be thinking about as we age?[3] It is not that we have arrived— the journey continues on from maturity to maturity and glory to glory. We will deal with issues such as being clear about our destination, direction, motive, passion, convictions, and purpose in life (knowing Jesus and becoming like Him in love, wisdom, and holiness).

Spiritual habits are the focus in Section 2. How should we maintain those disciplines (understood as habits of responsiveness to God's grace that "bring us into more effective cooperation with Christ and his Kingdom")[4] that are essential for developing Christian maturity? Old age should not be a season for apathy and laziness. It need not be a period of "institutionalised sloth",[5] but a time of studying God's Word, cultivating regular prayer, and growing habits of worship, participation in community, and service. Old age can be a richly fulfilling stage of our lives.

Section 3 is about the relationships in our lives. We are made for relationships, and in old age this becomes even more obvious and necessary. We will examine what makes us human, how we should focus on family and friends, and how to engage in conversations that are redemptive and edifying.

Section 4 brings us to the frailties, pain, and suffering of old age. We need to examine this part of our lives in a realistic way, not becoming pessimistic but learning how to manage our growing weaknesses in a biblical way. How can we come to terms with declining health and pain and suffering, with bereavement and loneliness, depression, and the fear of losing our memories?

The final section turns our attention to our eternal home—heaven. We will not live long on earth, but heaven will be our permanent address. It is important that we think more and more about where we are heading. How will we end our earthly lives? What will heaven be like? How can we prepare for it? While we wait, how can we harbour a living hope in our hearts amid advancing age, and how can we continue to be a blessing to others and leave a legacy that glorifies God?

Our churches are becoming filled with a growing population of seniors. People talk about a "silver tsunami" in many societies globally. This is also happening in church. Many churches are so focused on the young and young families (who are important concerns) that they neglect the concerns and needs of the seniors, who in many places feel left out and redundant. Many seniors can empathise with the characters in Gordon MacDonald's novel, *Who Stole My Church?* [6] MacDonald, writing in his old age, tries to express how many elderly Christians feel marginalised at church services; strangers in their own churches. This must change.

There are also older people who find it difficult to age well in a society that tends to deny the natural process of ageing. They may be tempted to maintain an illusion that they are immune to this most essential of human processes, "one that can be denied only with great harm".[7]

This book intends to raise issues connected with the spirituality of ageing and ministry to seniors. It is meant for seniors as well as church leaders and younger people who ought to be thinking about how to minister to the ageing. The chapters are kept short for easy reading, and the text is in large print to make it easier for older people to read! The chapters adopt a devotional format to encourage biblical study as well as practical application. There are questions intended for both personal reflection and group discussion.

The great Christian novelist George Macdonald wrote, "Age is not all decay; it is the ripening, the swelling, of the fresh life within, that withers and bursts the husk."[8] May that be our experience as we turn to Christ and stay with Him in old age as He strengthens and blesses us, filling our lives with His peace, joy, and love.

Robert M. Solomon

Part I:

A SPIRITUAL JOURNEY

Remembering Origins
and Destination

In his old age, the celebrated German theologian Friedrich Schleiermacher (1768–1834), known as the "father of modern liberal theology", was a pathetic sight. One day, he was sitting on a bench in a city park when a policeman, mistaking him for a tramp, shook him awake, asking, "Who are you?" With great sadness, Schleiermacher replied, "I wish I knew."[9] He was an intelligent and famous man, but his Christian faith had withered over the years.

Compare Schleiermacher to another old man—the apostle Paul who, in his old age, wrote from prison, "I know whom I have believed, and am convinced that he is able to guard what I have entrusted to him until that day" (2 Timothy 1:12). Earlier, Paul referred to God as the one "to whom I belong and whom I serve" (Acts 27:23). What a difference between a man who knew his identity and destiny and one who had forgotten.

Any proper narrative about our origins and destiny must be *rooted in God*. He is the one who created us, gives meaning and life to us, and is our highest goal. A life that is not rooted in God, as revealed in Christ, is bound to be blown around by the winds of circumstance and fickle fortune. It is like a kite that has lost its attachment to the kite-flyer. Paul knew where he came from and where he was going and knew that it is in God that "we live and move and have our being" (Acts 17:28). To forget or ignore God is to be like a fish that is removed from the sea. It wriggles, crying out for oxygen, and eventually dies.

It is easy to forget where we have come from and where we are going in a world that distracts and preoccupies us so easily. A pilot once found that some of the instruments in his plane had suddenly stopped working. He lost his bearings and was not able to tell where he was heading. He managed to contact a control tower on the ground, and when asked to give his position so that they could direct him to the nearest airport, he replied, "I don't know, but wherever I am headed, I am making it in good time!"

The pilot knew he had speed, but he had lost his sense of direction. How true this is of so many people today. Life moves quickly, but people have lost their inner direction. They have forgotten where they are headed and what their ultimate end would be. They know how to use their clocks, but what is the point if they have lost their compass? The world is a spiritual wilderness where it is easy to get lost without a moral and spiritual compass to guide us and point us in the right direction.

There are many who have never thought seriously about their final destination. They are quite happy to fill life with small goals, like what to buy, where to go for a holiday, what car to drive, and what clothes to wear. But these will amount to nothing if the big journey and goal in life are forgotten. The Lord Jesus once told His listeners, "So do not worry, saying, 'What shall we eat?' or 'What shall we drink?' or 'What shall we wear?' For the pagans run after all these things, and your heavenly Father knows that you need them. But seek first his kingdom and his righteousness, and all these things will be given to you as well" (Matthew 6:31–33).

If you have the big purpose in life clear, all the little goals will fall into place. Without the big picture, it is so easy to lose your way. It is possible that some start well, knowing where they are heading, but the pleasures of life, the entertainments along the way, and all the attendant worries and anxieties eventually draw them off their original path. They have lost their way and forgotten their ultimate destination.

There is always hope. If you have lost your way or neglected your ultimate destination, you can always do something about it. Return to God. People are urged to "Give careful thought to your ways" (Haggai 1:5, 7). The runway, so to speak, gets shorter as we age, and we must make sure we know where we will land. We must remember that ageing "is more important as a spiritual than a biological process".[10]

Jesus taught that our ultimate destination is the heavenly Father's house (John 14:1–3). That ultimate destiny is possible only if we place our faith in Christ and learn to live in Him while we are on earth. May we learn to say with Paul, "I press on towards the goal to win the prize for which God has called me heavenwards in Christ Jesus" (Philippians 3:14). This is the only destination that is worth living and dying for, the only one that offers eternal life. All others are dead ends.

Reflect

- How would you answer the question, "Where do you come from and where are you going?" If you find it difficult to answer the question, why is this so?

- How can a person in their senior years keep the ultimate Christian destination in sight? What would be the signs that this is happening? What would be difficulties, distractions, and temptations that one may face?

Staying
on the Way

In John Bunyan's classic book *Pilgrim's Progress,* the protagonist, Christian, travels from the City of Destruction (representing the sinful world) to the Celestial City (heaven).[11] Along the way, he encounters various difficulties and temptations. There are times when he is tempted to leave the way he has been directed to travel, either because of difficulties and obstacles, or because alternate paths provide an easier and nicer route. Bunyan is spot-on in pointing out the reasons why Christians are tempted to leave the narrow way they have to travel. These have to do with Satan's key methods to lead Christians astray, which are mirrored in the way the world often impedes our journey to heaven.

Satan is a master in using either seduction or threats to get people off the King's Highway to heaven. In

Pilgrim's Progress, the pilgrims find themselves in a town called Vanity Fair, where all kinds of things are on sale: merchandise, pleasure, fame, amusements, and the like. The pilgrims are urged to buy what is on offer, but they decline, for which they are imprisoned, and one is even martyred. Eventually, Christian escapes the clutches of this wicked place to continue his journey.

It may be good to remember that Abraham was a tent-dweller for the rest of his life after God called him to leave his home in Ur. Even after arriving in the Promised Land, he still dwelt in his tents. As the Bible says: "By faith he made his home in the promised land like a stranger in a foreign country; he lived in tents, as did Isaac and Jacob, who were heirs with him of the same promise. For he was looking forward to the city with foundations, whose architect and builder is God" (Hebrews 11:9–10). His ultimate goal was to reach God's heaven; thus although he arrived at an earthly address, he never lost sight of the fact that he was in fact a foreigner and stranger on earth (Hebrews 11:13) until he reached the better country, "a heavenly one" (Hebrews 11:16).

Our permanent address is not on earth, but in heaven. We can never settle down anywhere in the world and consider it our ultimate destination. We may enjoy peace, comfort, and prosperity for a while, but these things should never lead us to ignore our real ongoing journey. We forget this at our peril. It is good to sing this song regularly: "This world is not my home, I'm just a passing through. If heaven's not my home, then Lord what will I do?"

If seduction does not work, then Satan will use threats to get us off the path that leads to true life. In *Pilgrim's Progress*, Apollyon (Satan) blocks the path, commanding Christian to turn back or face his fury. Christian battles with Apollyon and is helped by God's angels. For centuries, Satan has been getting Christians to abandon the way of the Lord through both deception and danger, seduction and suffering.

Before he was martyred, Paul wrote from prison about how Demas had deserted him "because he loved this world" (2 Timothy 4:10). Paul also referred to others who had deserted him (2 Timothy 1:15; 4:16)—and by inference the faith—possibly because they did not want to endanger their own lives by being associated with Paul. How easily Satan can dislodge Christians from their journey to God. He can appear as an "angel of light" to deceive (2 Corinthians 11:14) or a "roaring lion" to intimidate (1 Peter 5:8). In either case, we must take the faithful posture of "standing firm" (1 Peter 5:9; Ephesians 6:14). We must stand firm and let nothing move us (1 Corinthians 15:58)—not the seductions of the devil and the world, nor the threats from them. Instead, *we must keep to the path if we are to reach God's heaven.*

G. K. Chesterton, the great English writer, observes wisely in *What's Wrong with the World* (1910):

> Man has always lost his way. He has been a tramp ever since Eden; but he always knew, or thought he knew, what he was looking for. Every man has a house somewhere in the elaborate cosmos; his house waits for him waist deep in slow Norfolk rivers or sunning itself upon Sussex downs. Man has always been looking for that home which is the subject matter of this book. But in the bleak and blinding hail of scepticism to which he has been now so long subjected, he has begun for the first time to be chilled, not merely in his hopes, but in his desires. For the first time in history he begins really to doubt the object of his wanderings on the earth. He has always lost his way; but now he has lost his address.[12]

It is easy to lose our way in this distracting and dangerous world. The greatest danger, perhaps, to the pilgrim's journey is what I would call "spiritual amusement parks." In amusement parks, people pay to get on rides; the faster the ride, the more exciting and entertaining it is. These rides give us a sense of travelling fast, but in the end we go nowhere; we merely return to where we started. With our sense of exhilaration rising and dying quickly, we move from one ride to the other, seeking endless entertainment. Could it be that Christians today face the temptation of entering spiritual amusement parks for exciting rides to nowhere? Instead these "amusement parks" become dangerous distractions, deceiving us into thinking we are going somewhere, confusing Disneyland rides for spiritual journeys.

We do well to bear in mind the wise warning of *The Shepherd of Hermas* (written between the end of the first and the mid-second century) of how not to grow old:

> Because your spirit is now old and withered up, and has lost its power in consequence of your infirmities and doubts. For, like elderly men who have no hope of renewing their strength, and expect nothing but their last sleep, so you, weakened by worldly occupations, have given yourselves up to sloth, and have not cast your cares upon the Lord. Your spirit therefore is broken, and you have grown old in your sorrows.[13]

The words of the psalmist speak to us powerfully: "You're blessed when you stay on course, walking steadily on the road revealed by GOD. You're blessed when you follow his directions, doing your best to find him. That's right—you don't go off on your own; you walk straight along the road he set. You, GOD, prescribed the right way to live; now you expect us to live it (Psalm 119:1–4 The Message). Indeed, "older age can be the beginning of our closest encounter with God"[14]—if we learn to stay with Christ.

Reflect

- Reflect on the two strategies that Satan and the sinful world use to lead Christians off course. What is your own experience of facing these challenges and overcoming them?

- What does staying on course look like for a Christian in his or her senior years? What would you say to those who seem to have gone off course?

Keeping the
Motive Clear

There is a story about Sir Christopher Wren, a celebrated English architect and builder, who designed and built the magnificent St Paul's Cathedral in the 17th century. He went to the construction site in disguise and talked to the workers there, asking each of them, "What are you doing?" One man said, "I am cutting a piece of stone." Another man replied, "I am earning five shillings two pence a day." A third worker warmed Wren's heart when he replied, "I am helping Sir Christopher Wren build a beautiful cathedral."[15]

The first man gave a technical answer, the second man an economic one, but it was the third man whose motive for his labour was outstanding, embracing a larger vision of glory.

Why do we do the things we do every day? Different people may have different reasons for their actions. They may be doing the same things, but their motives may be very different. Even things done in the name of Christian piety may be performed with the wrong motives. Take, for instance, the Pharisees at the time of Jesus. They were criticised by Jesus for practising a theatrical religion that was intended to impress observers. They performed their religious duties to be seen by others (Matthew 6:1, 5, 16).

Jesus did not condemn their pious acts per se, but their wicked and self-centred motivations. It is possible to do the right things but for the wrong reasons. This is how those who approach Jesus with their impressive religious acts (prophesying, driving out demons, and performing many miracles in the name of Jesus) will discover that their motives are wanting (Matthew 7:22–23). Jesus will call them "evildoers", not because they did evil things but because they tried to do good with evil motives. They did not do these things for the right reasons—for the glory of God and the good of others. Rather, they did it for their own glory and reputation.

God judges deeply and is not only focused on what we do, but also our motives. "All a person's ways seem pure to them, but motives are weighed by the LORD" (Proverbs 16:2). God's judgement will be comprehensive and include the purposes behind our actions, even those that seem so reasonable and noble on the surface.

The Shorter Westminster Catechism begins by stating a central Christian motive in life: "Man's chief end is to glorify God, and to enjoy him forever." This echoes what we read in the Bible: "So whether you eat or drink or whatever you do, do it all for the glory of God" (1 Corinthians 10:31). One may ask (quite rightly), "What has eating and drinking got to do with the glory of God?" To understand what Paul wrote here, we must examine its context. Paul was giving pastoral advice on the sensitive matter of whether Christians in the early church could eat meat offered to idols in pagan temples and later sold in the meat markets. Earlier, in 1 Corinthians 8, Paul referred to those who knew that idols were nothing and therefore how they were free to eat such meat offered to nothing.

However, eating such meat with the wrong motive—to show off one's supreme knowledge or the exercise of one's freedom—is not acceptable. For Paul, these were wrong reasons for doing so. The motive of love towers over that of knowledge and freedom. One eats or refrains from eating out of consideration for those with a weaker conscience. To avoid becoming a stumbling block to the faith of others is to exercise love—and such motives glorify God, because God is love (1 John 4:8). "If we love one another, God lives in us and his love is made complete in us" (v. 12).

We can do things—even good things—with less than noble motives. We can do things out of anger, pride, covetousness, to earn a false reputation, or the praise of men. Paul refused to judge his own actions on the basis of popularity, human praise, or even the comforting assurance of his own conscience. Instead he wrote a sobering thought: "Therefore judge nothing before the appointed time; wait until the Lord comes. He will bring to light what is hidden in darkness and *will expose the motives of the heart*. At that time each will receive their praise from God" (1 Corinthians 4:5, emphasis added).

How will we stand one day in the presence of God? Will we hear Him say, "Well done, good and faithful servant" (Matthew 25:21, 23)? Or, will we hear the terrifying words, "You wicked, lazy servant" (Matthew 25:26)? What God will say to us depends on what we have done but also *why* we did it—or why we failed to do something good. Our motives must be clean and godly, coming from a "a pure heart and a good conscience and a sincere faith" (1 Timothy 1:5). And this is possible only if we have a *growing relationship* with Jesus. We don't want Him to say, "I never knew you" (Matthew 7:23).

Therefore, let us pray the psalmist's prayer: "Search me, God, and know my heart; test me and know my anxious thoughts. See if there is any offensive way in me, and lead me in the way everlasting" (Psalm 139:23–24). Amid many distractions and motives, may God give us "an undivided heart" (Psalm 86:11) and a purity of heart that "wills one thing."[16]

Reflect

. . . .

- Read Isaiah 6:3. What do you think is the connection between God's holiness and His glory? How would you define God's glory? What does it mean to glorify God?

- How can our good deeds bring glory to God (Matthew 5:16)? How can we ensure that our actions are done with godly motives? What lesser motives must we guard ourselves against?

Keeping the
Passion Strong

American poet T. S. Eliot emphasised in his writings the importance of passion in our lives. But what is passion? Eliot mentions the difficulty of explaining the word to the uninitiated: "It is obvious that we can no more explain a passion to a person who has never experienced it than we can explain light to the blind."[17] It is not so easy to get the unpassionate to understand.

Passion is not mere physical energy; if that was the case, the older you grow, the less passion you will have. Passion, instead, refers to a spiritual fire that resides in the heart. The Bible uses various words to describe it, among which is "zeal". The Lord Jesus showed zeal throughout His life. It was zeal that kept twelve-year-old Jesus in the temple in deep discussion with the religious teachers, while His parents headed home (Luke 2:43–50). It was that same zeal for His Father's house that made Jesus clear out all those who had turned the temple into a marketplace, and this happened at the beginning of His public ministry (John 2:14–17), and also at the end (Matthew 21:12–13).

When He was tired and hungry, Jesus referred to an inner hunger that showed His zeal for His Father's will. "'My food,' said Jesus, 'is to do the will of him who sent me and to finish his work'" (John 4:34). He relentlessly headed to the cross of Calvary, ready to shed blood and sacrifice himself for the redemption of the world. We traditionally refer to His final sufferings, crucifixion, and death as the "passion of Christ". The week that commemorates these events every year is called Passion Week. Before His arrest, Jesus prayed to His Father, "I have brought you glory on earth by finishing the work you gave me to do" (John 17:4).

And on the cross, Jesus declared, amid painful gasps for air, "It is finished," and died so that we may live (John 19:30). This is what spiritual passion looks like, modelled for us by no less than the Son of God himself.

Those who follow Christ will display a similar passion. Take Paul, for instance. He was a man with great zeal; some say he was choleric by nature, a man who was driven by inner convictions. Before he met Christ, his zeal was misdirected against the young church. His passion for his Jewish faith blinded him from recognising who Jesus was, and he used his energy to persecute and arrest Christians (Acts 9:1–2; 26:9–11). The words "convinced" and "so obsessed" in Acts 26:9–11 help us understand Paul's misdirected passion.

After meeting the risen Christ, however, Paul's foundation and direction in life changed dramatically. His zeal remained undiminished—only now it was for the Lord and the mission He had entrusted to Paul. Immediately after his conversion Paul began to preach that Jesus is the Son of God (Acts 9:20). Tirelessly, he embarked on several arduous missionary journeys to spread the good news of Jesus Christ throughout the ancient Mediterranean world. He declared with great zeal, "It has always been my ambition to preach the gospel where Christ was not known" (Romans 15:20).

At the end of his life, Paul declared triumphantly, "I have fought the good fight, I have finished the race, I have kept the faith" (2 Timothy 4:7). Here was a man whose zeal never waned, remaining strong to the end.

It is possible to start well, with lots of zeal and enthusiasm. But as we age, we can lose much of it for various reasons. It is interesting to note that the kingdom of Judah had a number of good kings who in their senior years faltered and lost their original passion, backsliding (2 Chronicles 16; 20:31–37; 24:17–25; 25:14–28; 26:16–21; 32:24–31). All of them—Asa, Jehoshaphat, Uzziah, Joash, Amaziah, and Hezekiah—were commended at the beginning of their reigns for doing "what was good and right in the eyes of the LORD" (2 Chronicles 14:2). But all of them were like this only in their earlier years, or when their spiritual mentors were still around. *All of them declined spiritually in their senior years.*

In most of them, pride replaced humility and faith when they grew powerful. The story of Uzziah is most telling: "But after Uzziah became powerful, his pride led to his downfall" (2 Chronicles 26:16). It is good to be aware of the "vices of ageing" and how old sins can reappear in new forms in our later years.[18]

These kings lost their original passion as zealous reformers when they grew arrogant and started trusting in their own power, strategies, and alliances.

We must be careful not to lose our spiritual passion as we age; it is so easy for that to happen. What Jesus told the church in Ephesus—"You have forsaken the love you had at first"—continues to challenge us (Revelation 2:4). We are reminded that true spiritual passion has to do with our love for the Lord. Old age should not see this love decreasing. Our physical energies may diminish, but we must never equate decreasing energy with decreasing zeal for the Lord.

Paul's pastoral advice is most important in old age: "Never be lacking in zeal, but keep your spiritual fervour, serving the Lord" (Romans 12:11). We must do so right to the end. Perhaps spiritual writer James Houston was right in saying that retirement is "not in the language of the Christian".[19] Though we may be retired from gainful employment, we never really retire from walking with Christ and serving in His name—which we must do with undiminished passion. We would do well to remember that we do not retire from life but "re-fire into new life."[20]

Reflect

. . . .

- Recall the passion that you may have had in your early years as a Christian. What do you think true zeal for the Lord looks like? Make a list and examine your life in the light of your prayerful reflections.

- What are some reasons for the loss of spiritual passion among older Christians? Make a list of reasons and reflect on how this loss has happened, be it gradually or quickly. How can you prevent this from happening in your own life?

Being with Jesus

Several years ago, a Malaysian friend shared with me about a Chinese Coordination Centre of World Evangelism (CCCOWE) session for pastors in Kuala Lumpur. At the meeting, the general secretary, Dr Joshua Ting, shared "how the Chinese are good at knowing (pursuit of knowledge) and doing but lacking in the being (the personal relationship with Christ)." Dr Ting is spot on in his observation, and what he said is true for most Christians, regardless of ethnicity. In addition, more fundamental to *being* is our call to *being* with Christ.

Often, our identity is closely linked with our jobs, achievements, possessions, and roles.[21] In our old age, these things will have to be reviewed. So many of the things that gave meaning to our lives when we were younger will have changed in our old age.[22] The modern world has been infected by "affluenza", says psychologist Oliver James, who defines the "affluenza virus" as a set of values that involves "placing a high value on acquiring money and possessions, looking good in the eyes of others and wanting to be famous".[23] By this definition, many have been infected, including Christians, who may only realise it in their old age.

Many Christians believe in the modern pragmatic philosophy that our identity involves what we do. That is why when we meet strangers, we ask for their name and occupation. As a corrective to this deficient philosophy, we could turn to the classical and medieval philosophy that our identity has to do with who we are. The Bible, on the other hand, points to a different place to find our identity. It depends on *whose we are*, or *who we are with*.

Why is it that Christians shy away from finding our identity in being God's children and Christ's disciples? We tend to ignore or forget that eternal life is defined as knowing God the Father and the Son (John 17:3). This knowledge of God is essentially *relational*—it has to do with how we come to know a person. But the sinful human heart tends to reduce God to an "it", a habit that began in the Garden of Eden when Satan promised the knowledge of good and evil if Adam and Eve ate the forbidden fruit (Genesis 3:5). Satan had deftly distorted true knowledge and reduced it to factual knowledge. He injected a big lie into the thinking processes of the human race by saying that the purpose of life is to know *something*.

This directly contrasted with what God, the Creator, had designed. The purpose of life is to know *Someone*. God brought Adam and Eve together for them to know each other, and He visited them daily for walks (Genesis 3:8). We were made to walk with God and to know Him relationally. But because of their sin, Adam and Eve hid from God (and from each other). Since then, human beings have tended to ignore relational knowledge in their pursuit of informational knowledge. This can be seen in many forms, even with piety. Jesus challenged the Pharisees that despite knowing all the details of the Law, they had ignored the Lawgiver and did not know Him. They had bought Satan's lie that knowing something is more important than knowing someone.

Those who are turned off by the idea of becoming religious eggheads may instead be attracted to a form of false piety: endless activism. Theirs is a breathless form of Christianity; their frantic busyness hiding their lack of relational depth. W. H. Griffith Thomas was right when he said, "We cannot make up for failure in our devotional life by redoubling energy in service."[24] And yet, many Christians seem to be on a spiritual treadmill, wondering why they are not making any progress in their knowledge of God and His ways. Silence (Habakkuk 2:20) and stillness (Psalm 46:10) are good antidotes to mindless busyness in the Christian world.

Jesus described how we will be judged at the end. There will be many who rely on their doctrinal knowledge and their list of religious achievements to get past God's judgment seat. But they will be sorely disappointed (Matthew 7:21–27). Some will take pride in their knowledge of Scripture. And Scripture does say that *"everyone* who calls on the name of the LORD will be saved" (Joel 2:32, emphasis added). But how easily we turn Scriptural truths into superficial mantras! We become presumptuous and are easily misled. Thus, Jesus said, *"Not everyone* who says to me 'Lord, Lord,' will enter the kingdom of heaven" (Matthew 7:21, emphasis added). He was not contradicting Scripture but challenging the kind of Scripture reading that is merely informative rather than deeply formative.

Jesus also said that many who claim to have been busy doing good things (e.g., prophesying, exorcising, and doing miracles) in His name will be turned away from His kingdom because they had missed the most important truth: they had failed to be with Jesus. "I never knew you" (Matthew 7:23) is a divine statement that exposes the lack of a relationship between busy servants and their Master, and turns all their apparently good deeds to evil deeds!

Because the Lord has made it clear, we cannot claim ignorance or ask to be excused. Instead, we must learn to, first and foremost, spend unhurried time to know Jesus, listen to His voice, marvel at His character, discover His will, understand His ways, and enjoy His presence. Then our quest for knowledge and desire to do good will find fulfilment in the light of our being with Jesus. Then we can avoid ending up with heads crammed with information and schedules filled with activities, but hearts empty of God. We will discover that the most profound thing to say at the end of life is not "I thought" or "I did", but "I loved".

Reflect

· · · · · · · · · ·

- Assess how much of your life is lived according to the various philosophies mentioned in the chapter (doing, being, being with). Why is "being with" the most important?

- Read Mark 3:13–15. Jesus called His disciples "that they might *be with* him and that he might *send* them out to preach." What are the implications for modern-day disciples? How does an ageing senior practise being with Christ?

Becoming Christlike

What is God's central purpose for His people? That was the question John Stott spent many years trying to answer. He explored various answers, but finally found one that brought him deep satisfaction. He wrote about it in his last book, *The Radical Disciple*: "*God wants his people to become like Christ,* for Christlikeness is the will of God for the people of God" (emphasis added).[25]

Many other Christian writers and theologians agree. For example, Eugene Peterson asserts: "The goal for Christians is God's work of salvation and the means is Jesus."[26] Likewise, the many writings of Dallas Willard (*The Divine Conspiracy, The Great Omission, The Renovation of the Heart*) underline this point. Willard defines sanctification as "the process of forming the inner world of the human self in such a way that it takes on the character of the inner being of Jesus himself."[27]

This point is emphasised in Scripture. We read in Romans 8:29: "For those God foreknew he also predestined *to be conformed to the image of his Son*" (emphasis added). The purpose of our salvation is for us to bear the likeness of Christ. We may have to question our salvation if we are not growing in Christlikeness.

Many years ago, I was invited to the birthday party of a wealthy man. The organisers of the party gave each guest a mask in the likeness of the man's face to be worn before he arrived. When the unsuspecting man stepped out of his car, he nearly died of shock as he saw a sea of masks resembling his face.

Later, I reflected on this incident and wondered if hell would be like that—would it be a place where one wakes up to see nothing but his own face? Would God condemn self-centred people to an eternity of being surrounded by themselves? I believe that would be a terrible torment.

Conversely, would heaven be a place where we wake up and are surrounded by the face of Christ? Of course, heaven is where the Lamb of God will take central place. But is it also not true that those who dwell in heaven will look like Christ? If God's purpose is fulfilled and God's promise that when Christ returns, "we shall be like him" (1 John 3:2) is accomplished, will not heaven's residents bear a family resemblance to the Son of God? Heaven would be heaven because we will see Christ everywhere—including on the faces of the redeemed.

Because this is true, we need to ensure that we are growing in Christlikeness, even as we continue to grow in age. The more time passes, the more we should resemble Christ in our character—in holiness, love, compassion, justice, wisdom, patience, gentleness, and so on. In Scripture, we read about the fruit of the Spirit (Galatians 5:22–23), which is in fact, the very character of Christ. As the Holy Spirit dwells in us and helps us to bear fruit, we will grow in Christlikeness. It is a process that is enabled by God's grace and power.

In Psalm 115:8, we read that those who make idols and trust in them will *be like them*. The principle is that whatever you look at regularly will be what you end up looking like. This may explain why many couples tend to look alike over time, or why in pet-master lookalike competitions, a man may look like his bulldog or a woman like her cat. And perhaps, this is also why folk wisdom is reflected when we say so-and-so is money-faced. If you keep looking at money, you will end up looking like it!

This principle is also true in our spiritual journey. The more we look at Jesus, the more we will grow to be like Him. It is no surprise that Scripture exhorts us to run the race "fixing our eyes on Jesus" (Hebrews 12:2). We need to say with the psalmist, "My eyes are ever on the LORD" (Psalm 25:15), "to gaze on the beauty of the LORD" (Psalm 27:4).

How can we do this? When we read the Bible, especially the Gospels, and contemplate who Christ is, what He said, and what He did, and seek to emulate Him, then we are keeping our eyes on Him. As we do so, we will be transformed into His likeness in increasing measure. "And we all, who with unveiled faces contemplate the Lord's glory, are being transformed into his image with ever-increasing glory, which comes from the Lord, who is the Spirit" (2 Corinthians 3:18).

To stand at the gates of heaven with a resemblance to Christ will be a kind of passport, evidence that we have been saved by His grace and sanctified, and that we belong to God's family in heaven.

Reflect

. . . .

- Would you agree that Christlikeness is God's highest purpose for His people? Make a list of what would characterise Christlikeness. Assess your own progress in this area, and the possible reasons for your progress, or lack thereof.

- What does it mean to keep our eyes fixed on Jesus? How does worldliness and temptation take our eyes off Jesus? How does ageing influence the way we keep our eyes on Jesus? Think about people who show more of Christ as they age. What do you think is their secret?

Strengthening
Convictions

A father whose son suffered a medical condition involving the brain came to me for counsel. The son had undergone surgery to relieve pressure on the brain and was missing part of his skull as a result. Sometime later, consideration was given to performing another surgery to close up the gap. Different doctors gave differing advice, and the father was confused. He narrowed down his choice of surgeon to two doctors: the one who had done the first surgery and another doctor who had been consulted for a second opinion.

The second doctor seemed very confident—a bit too confident. The first doctor was a quieter man, but he seemed to know what he was doing. The rest of the family preferred the first doctor, but the man was drawn to the second. However, he later discovered certain information that the second doctor had withheld from him, and decided to go with the first.

How do we assess someone who shows confidence in their beliefs or opinions? Is it possible for one's strong convictions to be misplaced? When we Christians hold onto our convictions, how do we ensure we are not blindly or stubbornly making a mistake?

When God promised Abraham in his old age that he would have a son, it is said that Abraham was "*fully convinced* that God was able to do what he had promised" (Romans 4:21, emphasis added), though he was close to a hundred years old. It was this faith in God that was credited as righteousness in Abraham's life.

Paul too, was a man who lived according to his convictions. In discussing our present sufferings and future glory, Paul wrote how he was *fully convinced* nothing in creation can separate us from the love of God in Christ (Romans 8:38–39). Paul did not lose this conviction even when facing execution for preaching about Christ. At the end of his life, he wrote with undiminished confidence, "The Lord will rescue me from every evil attack and will bring me safely to his heavenly kingdom" (2 Timothy 4:18). His faith in God and His promises never wavered even in the most difficult of circumstances.

This brings us to an important point. True Christian convictions must be rooted in our knowledge of God and His Word. The more we know God, the more we will be convinced that God loves us and is sovereign over our lives. The more we know His Word, the more we will be convinced that God will keep all His promises and will bring us safely to heaven, no matter what difficulties we currently face.

But why is it that some Christians lose their Christian convictions? It could be that suffering and pain, while drawing some people closer to God, may tempt others to move away from Him. They could have wrongly believed that the Christian life promises nothing but comfort and prosperity, and when things become difficult, they grow disappointed and drift away from God.

Others may suffer from weak convictions because they never really studied God's Word and built their lives on biblical convictions in the first place. They just drifted along in worldliness, peppered with weekly doses of dutiful churchgoing. Worsening health and a sense of approaching death may also make some people question their long-held Christian convictions.

Growing maturity means that some of our beliefs will become stronger and others may be held more lightly.

Godly wisdom will enable us to know the difference. Those convictions that are derived from knowing God and His Word must remain firm and grow stronger. These have to do with who God is, our salvation in Christ, His eternal kingdom where we will be blessed with eternal life, our call to become Christlike through the sanctifying work of the Holy Spirit, and our labour in the Lord not being in vain.

But there are also some convictions that we may hold, drawn from our misreading of Scripture or from popular Christian beliefs (that we will be rewarded in heaven with mansions, for example), that can be laid aside as we grow in our knowledge of God and His Word. As we grow older, we must know the difference between non-negotiable beliefs (e.g., that Christ is fully God and fully human) and those that are really nothing more than opinion.

Stubbornly holding on to our opinions and giving up on those biblical beliefs which must be firmly held in our hearts and minds is dangerous. A former UN secretary general, Dag Hammarskjöld, recorded in his remarkable personal journal, "God does not die on the day we cease to believe in a personal deity, but we die on the day when our lives cease to be illumined by the steady radiance, renewed daily, of a wonder, the source of which is beyond all reason."[28]

It is not easy, living in a postmodern world where everything is seen as relative, and any claim to absolute truth is laughed at. For the ageing Christian, the end of life on earth should make us even bolder in our biblical beliefs and faith. With increasing age, we need to discover our vocation. That vocation, says David Maitland, is to learn "to become part of a counterculture".[29] In resisting the rush of contemporary society and practising countercultural biblical reflection on their lives and experience, seniors will increasingly sense that they are in the world but not of it.[30]

As Scripture exhorts us, we must "hold firmly to the faith we profess" (Hebrews 4:14) because our hope in Christ is "an anchor for the soul, firm and secure" (Hebrews 6:19). We need not drift, but can stand firmly on the biblical foundations of our faith.

Reflect

·········

- Make a list of your personal convictions upon which you live. Compare that list with the Apostles' Creed or the Nicene Creed. Which of your convictions are non-negotiable and which are beliefs you are not sure of? Share your reflections with other Christians.

- Why and how do people lose their convictions when they grow old? How would you help someone in this situation?

Growing Wise

The Desert Fathers were a group of monks who lived in the Egyptian desert whose teachings and stories have been collected. Here is the story of one of them, called Abba Moses.

> A brother in Scetis committed a fault. A council was called to which Moses was invited, but he refused to go to it. Then the priest sent someone to him, saying, "Come, for everyone is waiting for you". So he got up and went. He took a sack, filled it with sand and cut a small hole at the bottom and carried it on his shoulders. The others came out to meet him and said, "What is this, father." The Abba said to them, "My sins run out behind me, and I do not see them, and today I am

coming to judge the errors of another." When they heard that, they said no more to the brother but forgave him.[31]

The story, like many about the Desert Fathers, reflects their wisdom, honed by life in the desert and age. How does one grow in wisdom?

The Old Testament contains a few books that are collectively called Wisdom Literature. One of these books, the book of Proverbs, teaches practical wisdom centred on godliness. We learn that the "fear of the LORD is the beginning of knowledge, but fools despise wisdom and instruction" (Proverbs 1:7). Wisdom is personified as a woman and the reader is urged, "Do not forsake wisdom, and she will protect you; love her, and she will watch over you. The beginning of wisdom is this: get wisdom. Though it cost all you have, get understanding" (Proverbs 4:6–7).

The suffering Job, defending against the false accusations of his friends, asked, "Is not wisdom found among the aged? Does not long life bring understanding?" (Job 12:12). Old age should be marked by wisdom gained over the years. But where does this wisdom come from? In the next verse, Job declares, "To God belong wisdom and power; counsel and understanding are his" (Job 12:13).

This becomes clearer in the New Testament when Jesus

is described as the one "in whom are hidden all the treasures of wisdom and knowledge" (Colossians 2:3). Thus, Jesus "has become for us wisdom from God" (1 Corinthians 1:30). The people who listened to Jesus marvelled at His wisdom (Matthew 13:54; Mark 6:2) and His disciples treasured His wise teachings in their hearts, propagating them through their preaching and writing.

The followers of Jesus are expected to show the wisdom of Christ; we are exhorted to have the mind of Christ (Philippians 2:5). As such, those who minister in church and provide leadership are expected to be "full of the Spirit and wisdom" (Acts 6:3).

This wisdom from above is made available to all believers. James assures us: "If any of you lacks wisdom, you should ask God, who gives generously to all without finding fault, and it will be given to you" (James 1:5). Such heavenly wisdom must show itself in the way we live. "But the wisdom that comes from heaven is first of all pure; then peace-loving, considerate, submissive, full of mercy and good fruit, impartial and sincere" (James 3:17). It will reflect mature godliness and Christlikeness, being rooted in humility, which is an important mark of wisdom. Such wisdom in old age is worthy of respect. "Stand up in the presence of the aged, show respect for the elderly and revere your God. I am the LORD" (Leviticus 19:32). Wisdom should manifest itself among the old as reverence, temperance, dignity, sensibility, and soundness in faith, love, and perseverance (Titus 2:2–3).

The Lord Jesus told a parable to show the difference between a wise man and a foolish one (Matthew 7:24–27). Jesus declared: "Everyone who hears these words of mine and puts them into practice is like a wise man who built his house on the rock" (Matthew 7:24). His foolish neighbour also hears the words of Jesus but does not obey Him; he is like a man who builds his house on the sand (Matthew 7:26). Both houses looked similar to the untrained eye, but their profound difference was seen when the storms and floods came. One day, the rains poured heavily on both houses, the wild winds blew ferociously on them, and the rivers swelled menacingly. The house on the sand could not withstand this assault and collapsed with a "great crash" (Matthew 7:27).

It is possible for us to start off well. Our house is built on the right foundation—strong and sturdy. But things can go wrong. A person may have started out well and sought to live faithfully as a disciple of Christ. But over time, he may lose his faith as *doubt* (about the truth that the house on the rock is the only safe place) creeps in, or *distress* and suffering suggest that it is all not worth it, or when sinful *desires* take over as he sees what others outside the house on the rock seem to be enjoying. All these may change his ultimate end.

One of the stories in John Duckworth's witty book *Joan 'n' the Whale: And Other Stories You Never Heard in Sunday School* is "The Man Who Built His House Upon the Rock."[32] A man built his house upon a rock and congratulated himself for being wise. He waited for the rain, knowing that his neighbour's house on the sand would collapse. He waited for the storm warnings but they never came. Puzzled, he nevertheless continued waiting for the storm. He could hardly wait to see his neighbour's house fall, and for his neighbour to come begging for shelter. With such smug thoughts, he waited for the storm. He heard sounds of yelling and pounding one day and told himself excitedly that the day had come, only to be disappointed when he looked out the window. His neighbour was upgrading; he was converting his house into a beachfront resort.

The rain did come one day, but it fell only on the house that was built on the rock! The man moaned with dismay and busied himself with patching the roof, cleaning the gutters, and bailing out the basement. This went on for quite a while. The neighbour who built his house on the sand got wealthier, more successful, and happier. But the man whose house was on the rock was kept busy coping with a record rainfall that fell only on his house!

Finally the man gave up, saying, "Any fool can see that there's not going to be any storm." He packed up his belongings, moved out of his house, and went next door to the luxury beachfront resort. He said, "If you can't beat 'em, join 'em."

That night, of course, the rain descended, and the floods came, and the winds blew and beat upon both those houses. The one that was built upon the sand fell, and great was the fall of it. The other fell not; for it was founded upon a rock. Too bad nobody was home.

Is your house built on the rock? Are you still living in that house? If so, then you are wise.

How then can we grow in wisdom? We must realise that wisdom comes from God. Knowing Him is essential for growing in wisdom. Humility is the right attitude to have as we learn from God. Reading the Bible provides us with godly wisdom through perspectives and precepts for living. Obedience is central to growing in wisdom. The disobedient cannot expect to grow wise. Love is the key ingredient in wisdom. We grow wise as we learn to love

God and others in ways specific to our life circumstances. Connecting with the accumulated knowledge of Christians past and present will help us imbibe some of that wisdom. This comes through reading good Christian literature and engaging in deep spiritual conversations with mature Christians.

Reflect

- How would you characterise a Christian who is wise? How do you think he or she has grown wise?

- How did Jesus define a wise man? Is your house built on the rock? How then can we grow in wisdom?

Becoming
Loving

Dr Lewis Sperry, 19th century American theologian, was praying with his colleague, renowned Bible teacher Dr Harry Ironside, one day when he was startled to hear Ironside pray, "Lord, keep me from turning out to be a mean old man." Perhaps Ironside was aware of how the difficulties and complexities of ageing could make one deteriorate into irritability. God obviously answered his prayer because not only was he a kind and gracious man, he steadily remained so as he advanced in years.[33] Instead of prickliness, he was noted for his gentleness.

Love is central in our understanding of God, for we read in Scripture that God is love (1 John 4:8). God has poured this divine love into our hearts by the Holy Spirit (Romans 5:5), even as we repent and place our trust in Christ for our salvation. Because God has first loved us, we are able to love Him and others (1 John 4:19). This God-given love has both vertical (towards God) and horizontal (towards others) dimensions.

When asked what the greatest commandment was, Jesus summarised the Hebrew Bible (the Old Testament) with these words: "Love the Lord your God with all your heart and with all your soul and with all your mind . . . Love your neighbour as yourself" (Matthew 22:37–39). This should be the central mark of a disciple of Christ.

Our love for God will be evidenced by wholehearted devotion to God, with no place for any rivals of God in our hearts. This includes the sinful self which loves to sit on the heart's throne. The one clear sign that we love God is that we will obey Him without reservations. Jesus said, "If you love me, keep my commands" (John 14:15) and "Whoever has my commands and keeps them is the one who loves me" (John 14:21). A person who does not obey God cannot claim to love God. But a person whose love for God is growing will also demonstrate growing obedience.

Love is not just a sentimental feeling that we profess to God when we sing or worship. It is far deeper than that. Some have pointed out that love should be considered a verb—in that it is always expressed in action—and there is truth in that understanding.[34] If we say we love God, it is best expressed in our submission and obedience to God.

Love also has horizontal implications. If we really love God, we will also love those around us. The apostle John noted the strong connection between love for God and others. He challenged his readers, "Whoever claims to love God yet hates a brother or sister is a liar" (1 John 4:20). The apostle James calls this other-directed love the "royal law" (James 2:8), and the apostle Paul says it sums up the entire law (Romans 13:9; Galatians 5:14).

What does this love for others look like? We have many descriptions in the Bible, the most famous being Paul's great portrayal of love in 1 Corinthians 13. There, we read what love is not and what it is. Love is not self-centred. It is not boastful, proud, envious, revengeful, rude, or easily angered; it does not keep grudges or delight in evil. Instead, love aims for the good of others. It is kind, patient, and forgiving, always full of trust and hope; it therefore perseveres and will never fail.

Augustine in the fifth century described love this way: "What does love look like? It has the hands to help others. It has the feet to hasten to the poor and needy. It has eyes to see misery and want. It has the ears to hear the sighs and sorrows of men. That is what love looks like."[35] I would add, "That is what Christ looks like."

The Christian who grows in love will look more and more like Christ. He will have the eyes of Christ, who says to us, "I tell you, open your eyes and look at the fields! They are ripe for harvest" (John 4:35). We need to see others as Jesus saw them (Matthew 9:36): harassed (no rest), helpless (no power), and like sheep without a shepherd (no guidance).

We also need to have the ears of Jesus to hear the cries of the needy (Mark 10:47–49) and the heart of Jesus to see others with compassion (Matthew 9:36). We are, in the words of C. S. Lewis, "little Christs"[36] who show Him to others in how we relate with them.

We do not need to wait till we feel love, for love is more than an emotion; it is a commitment rooted in Christ. In his book *Mere Christianity*, C. S. Lewis wrote, "Do not waste your time bothering whether you 'love' your neighbor; act as if you did. As soon as we do this, we find one of the great secrets. When you are behaving as if you loved someone, you will presently come to love him. If you injure someone you dislike, you will find yourself disliking him more. If you do him a good turn, you will find yourself disliking him less."[37] Such love is divine in origin and is marked by selfless sacrifice and self-giving love.

There are people who need our love as we grow

in Christ. We need to realise that old age is "not a punishment but a privilege" and see beyond our own needs.[38] When we do this, we may notice that there are people around us who will appreciate our caring concern for them.

> Mamie Adams always went to a branch post office in her town because the postal employees there were friendly. She went there to buy stamps just before Christmas one year and the lines were particularly long. Someone pointed out that there was no need to wait in line because there was a stamp machine in the lobby. "I know," said Mamie, 'but the machine won't ask me about my arthritis.[39]

Is there not a message for all of us here?

Reflect

- Do you agree that love is often a verb? Make a list of how love acts in daily life. What personal implications are there for you?

- How can we show love for God? Imagine Jesus asking you the question He asked the apostle Peter three times: "Do you love me?" (John 21:15–19). What is your answer? How do you think Jesus would respond?

Part II:

SPIRITUAL HABITS

Reading the
Bible Deeply

I bet you don't know the Lord's Prayer," one man
challenged his friend.

"I bet I do!" the friend replied.

"I bet you a dollar you don't."

"I bet you five dollars I do."

"Okay, let's hear it."

"Now I lay me down to sleep. I pray the Lord my soul
to keep. If I should die before I wake, I pray the Lord my
soul to take."

"All right, here's your five dollars. I didn't know you
knew it."[40]

We may smile when we read this story about biblical
illiteracy among some Christians. Indeed, there are some
Christians who do not read the Bible regularly or have
not read the Bible at all. A disciple of Christ is one who

treasures the Word of God and reads it daily. He or she has a hunger for God's Word similar to our physical hunger for food. "Man shall not live on bread alone, but on every word that comes from the mouth of God" (Matthew 4:4). "But those who obey God's word truly show how completely they love him. That is how we know we are living in him" (1 John 2:5 NLT).[41]

The necessity of reading and meditating regularly on God's enduring Word was spelled out in God's instructions to Joshua in the Old Testament. "Study this Book of Instruction continually. Meditate on it day and night so you will be sure to obey everything written in it. Only then will you prosper and succeed in all you do" (Joshua 1:8 NLT).

The Bible describes itself as spiritual food that nourishes our souls, a light for our paths, a double-edged sword that exposes our sinfulness, a hammer that breaks our stubbornness, medicine that heals our wounds, and sweeter than honey to delight our spirits. To not read the Bible regularly is to miss all these blessings.

Yet, there are so many who neglect personal Bible-reading. The Bible is God's instruction book on how to be saved and live holy lives. It provides us with God's truth and principles for living. The more we read it, the more we understand God and His ways. But the Bible is also like a personal love letter to us. Through it, God speaks to our hearts in amazing ways, bringing His voice close to our ears. To not read the Bible regularly is like storing up letters sent by a loved one far away, unopened and unread. What a tragedy that would be!

Age should bring with it a growing familiarity with God's Word and a growing intimacy with God. We should be able to see the big picture narrative of the Bible, but also its specific parts and particular gems we have found in it—the unchanging truths that anchor our souls to God, the steady promises of God, and those places in the Bible where God has specifically spoken to us or ministered to us—creating faith, steadying our steps, giving us guidance, healing our wounds, encouraging and comforting us, or explaining mysteries.

We should have precious memories of our interaction with God's Word. Tom Meyer, a member of Wordsower International Ministries, is reputed to have memorised at least 20 books in the Bible and is able to recite them. He has been recruited by a Bible college to teach a course on Scripture memorisation.[42] Very few Christians can match Meyer's amazing feat, though in bygone days it was not unknown for Christians to have memorised big chunks of

Bible passages. With today's technological gadgets, people don't commit to memory many things, including Bible passages—and that is a great loss.

The psalmist told God, "I have stored up your word in my heart, that I might not sin against you" (Psalm 119:11 ESV). How can we store God's Word in our hearts unless we read it regularly, meditate on it deeply, and diligently memorise what we have read and discovered? Such remembering will help us in times of temptation and spiritual battle, as Jesus himself demonstrated when He quoted the Bible in response to Satan's temptation (Matthew 4:1–11) and overcame the evil one.

Storing God's Word in our hearts will also help us in times of crisis and trouble. When Jonah was swallowed by a big fish, his prospects for survival were pretty slim. Then he prayed to God. An examination of the prayer (Jonah 2) reveals that it is actually a collection of quotations from various psalms. Is it not possible that in his semi-conscious state, as he lay in the asphyxiating prison of a fish's stomach, the Spirit of God brought out what Jonah had read in God's Word from the depths of his memory and arranged them into a wonderful prayer? Is this not possible also for Christians facing their final moments on earth?

If you have not been reading God's Word deeply, it is

never too late to start doing so. Most seniors have more time on their hands, time that must be seriously invested in knowing God and His Word. Make it a daily habit to read God's Word. Read the whole Bible, a chapter or a few chapters at a time, or follow a Bible reading plan. Read prayerfully, with the intention of hearing God speak to you, and with the purpose of obeying God. Read the Bible with other Christians in a small group. Talk about what you have read. Learn to memorise key passages.

What is your relationship with God's Word? Does it abide in you? "Let the word of Christ dwell in you richly" (Colossians 3:16 ESV). Do you abide in it? Jesus said, "If you abide in my word, you are truly my disciples" (John 8:31 ESV). Does your personal Bible show any evidence that this is true?

Reflect

....

- Read the following passages about the Word of God: Psalm 119:103; Psalm 119:105; Proverbs 4:20–22; Jeremiah 23:29; John 8:32; John 17:17; Romans 10:17; Romans 15:4; Hebrews 4:12–13; Hebrews 5:12. What do they tell you about the importance of reading and meditating regularly on God's Word?

- What are some factors that hinder Bible reading and meditation? Why is obedience a vital part of getting deeper into God's Word?

Discovering the
Secrets of Prayer

In a *Peanuts* cartoon, Charlie Brown is kneeling beside his bed for prayer. Suddenly, he stops and says to Lucy, "I think I've made a new theological discovery, a real breakthrough. If you hold your hands upside down, you get the opposite of what you pray for."

We smile knowingly, for often people have the wrong idea of prayer. They turn it into a spiritual technique to make things happen, to get what they want. It was to dispel such notions that Jesus told His disciples not to find a model of prayer among the pagans, who "think they will be heard because of their many words" (Matthew 6:7). Neither were the disciples to look for a model among the Pharisees, who specialised in making prayer a matter of theatrics.

The disciples approached Jesus with the request, "Lord, teach us to pray" (Luke 11:1). Who better than Jesus to teach us about prayer? He was praying when the disciples approached Him. He prayed often and regularly; even on the cross He prayed to His Father. Jesus told His disciples that prayer was neither spiritual theatre nor spiritual technique. Rather, it is *a living and growing relationship.*

In teaching His disciples the Lord's Prayer (or the Disciple's Prayer, as some prefer to call it), Jesus highlighted the multiple facets of our relationship with God. We begin with our relationship to God as His children (Our Father). Then, the Prayer reminds us of the King and His subjects (Your kingdom come), the Master and His servants (Your will be done). Then, in turn, it deals with the relationship between the Benefactor and the beggar (Give us today our daily bread), the Saviour and the sinner (Forgive us), the Guide and the pilgrim (Lead us not into temptation), and the Defender and the helpless (Deliver us from evil).

The Lord's Prayer reveals to us that prayer is an expression of our relationship with God, and by praying, our relationship with Him grows. We learn to walk with God as we talk with Him. The language we use in prayer should be the language of love, as we thank God for His abiding love, entrust ourselves to Him, tell Him how much we love Him, and experience His presence daily.

But why is it that many do not find prayer an intimate experience? It may be because they are stuck in simplistic forms of prayer. They need to grow up in their prayer life.

In the childhood phase of prayer, we discover that *prayer is powerful*. This is usually the case early in the Christian life. In the heady days of such discovery, we realise that prayer can be a powerful tool. When we pray, things happen.

The danger arises when prayer is seen as an efficient technique to make things happen. Prayer, then, is like a remote control in our human hands. We press some buttons to move God and mobilise heaven. We tend to focus our attention on the remote control, the gadget in our hands. We think of making prayer more efficient and believe that this can be done by improving the techniques. It is easy in these circumstances for prayer to be mixed with superstition, as if changing the form of prayer can make it more powerful.

In the teenage phase of prayer, we begin to slowly realise that the remote control does not work as we think it should. It is not simply a matter of pressing some buttons to move heaven and change earth. We learn that *God is powerful*. We cannot dictate to Him what we want. He alone determines what to do and when to do it. Sometimes

He answers our prayers, and at other times He seems to ignore our pleas. He seems to be in total control. Disgusted and disappointed with our relative powerlessness and the ineffectiveness of the tool of prayer, we throw away the remote control and stop praying as fervently as we used to.

Then, we discover the wonderful truth that *God is love* (1 John 4:8). We enter the adult stage of prayer. Neither the maxim "prayer is powerful" nor the one that "God is powerful" are, on their own, sufficient to teach us about prayer. They tend to make us either obsessed with the techniques of praying in order to manipulate or appease God into working for us, or if He is too independent for our liking, give up praying altogether. Somewhere along the way, however, we realise that God is loving and He longs to speak to us and hear us speak the language of love. Prayer is the language of love, a language of intimacy.

We can pray because we are *driven* to God by our needs. But we can also pray because we are *drawn* by God's beauty and glory. To move from the former to the latter is to grow in prayer. Let us avoid treating prayer as a spiritual remote control. Let us instead turn our attention to God in true prayer. At His feet we will find heaven. In His voice, we will find true love. If only we realise that prayer is a loving relationship with God. As we pray, things may change—sometimes. But one thing is sure. As we pray, we will be changed. For God's love changes us.

Reflect

- Meditate on the Lord's Prayer. Pray it slowly, phrase by phrase, pausing in between phrases, and adding your own words. Why is the Lord's Prayer a deep lesson on our manifold relationship with God? Which part of the Prayer have you neglected the most, and how can you rectify that?

- Reflect on your life as a journey in prayer. What have been the high and low points in this journey? Where are you presently and what can you do to grow in prayer?

Hearing
God Afresh

A young man attended a Bible study where the pastor spoke about listening to God's voice and obeying Him. He left the church and drove home that night, wondering if God still spoke to His people. He prayed to God that if He still spoke, he would obey. On the way, he had a strong impression or urge to buy a bottle of milk. Ignoring it only made it stronger; so he bought the milk. As he passed a certain street, he felt God telling him to turn in there. Reluctantly, he turned and drove down a few blocks until he felt God telling him to stop.

When he stopped, again he felt God telling him to bring the milk to the house across the street. When he rang the bell, a surprised man opened the door to receive the milk. The man immediately ran to his wife who had a baby in hand. He shared with the young man how they had run out of money to feed the baby and had prayed that God would send an angel to help them. The young man gave them all the money he had and walked out into the street with tears in his eyes, convinced that God still speaks and answers prayers.[43]

Perhaps the events of our lives are not as dramatic as this story. God hardly speaks to us so clearly, and the last time you heard God speak may have been long ago. But do we not read in the Bible that God is a speaking God (Hebrews 1:1–3)? Samuel Williamson points out that hearing God is not just for spiritual giants, but for all God's children.[44] If so, why is it that many have a hard time hearing Him?

To be sure, there are some who seem to hear God all the time. At times, this borders on imagination more than actually hearing God. The Bible does warn against false prophets who "speak visions from their own minds, not from the mouth of the LORD" (Jeremiah 23:16). Nevertheless, God does still speak through impressions and gut feelings, as testified to by many Christians who are walking with the Lord. How then do we know if an impression we have is from God or from our own imagination or even from Satan? A book like Martin Wells Knapp's *Impressions* would be most helpful for deeper reflection on this.[45]

There are a few principles that can help us. First, God speaks mainly through His Word. The intimate connection between the Holy Spirit and the Word of God is something that was strongly emphasised by the Reformers and must not be treated lightly. It is when we read our Bibles that we hear God speaking to us. In the above story, notice the connection between the Bible study and the extraordinary experience of the young man.

Second, God will never contradict His Word when He speaks to us. If you hear a voice telling you to do something that goes against God's Word, you must be careful indeed.

Third, what God says to you must often be tested against what God is saying to other mature Christians.

There is a deeper challenge when it comes to hearing God. It has to do with our spiritual ears. A man was sharing with a friend how he was deaf in one ear, and asked him to sit next to his good ear so that he could hear him. He quipped that he turned his deaf ear towards his wife whenever he did not want to hear her nagging.

Could the problem be that we turn a deaf ear to God? We need God's grace to have spiritual ears that can hear Him speaking. We read in Psalm 40:6, "You have dug out two ears for me" (GOD'S WORD). The idea here is that

God fashions and creates spiritual ears that can listen to Him. Without this, we will be deaf to God.

Our ears also need regular awakening by God. "He wakens me morning by morning, wakens my ear to listen like one being instructed. The Sovereign LORD has opened my ears" (Isaiah 50:4–5). This is a wonderful experience as we are greeted by the Lord every morning. Just as our eyes open to the world when we wake up, our ears are also opened to hear the word from God. When we open the Bible to read, our opened ears are ready to hear what God wants to teach or show us.

The Hebrew word that is translated "like one being instructed" is *limmud*, which can be translated "disciple" as in Isaiah 8:16 ("seal up God's instruction among my disciples"). In other words, discipleship is possible only when our ears are opened by God and remain open to hear Him. Thus Jesus exhorts us, "consider carefully how you listen" (Luke 8:18). This means at least two things. Firstly, take care that you listen to God—through careful and prayerful reading of His Word. Secondly, make sure you obey God when He speaks to you.

Disobedience dulls our spiritual ears but obedience sharpens them. Age dulls our physical ears, but our spiritual hearing should remain keen. So then, how is your hearing?

Reflect

· · · · · · · · · · ·

- Read John 10. What do you think Jesus meant when He said that His sheep know His voice (v. 4) and listen to His voice (v. 3)? What is the connection between the two ideas? What are the personal implications for you?

- Read 2 Timothy 3:16–17; John 14:26; 17:17. Why is the Bible the primary means by which God speaks to us? If He speaks in other ways, how can we ascertain that it is God we are hearing?

Consecrating Life

In medieval times, as the gospel was brought to numerous European tribes, many turned to Christ and were baptised. There are stories of some tribes, like the Irish, who were willing to be baptised—but on one condition. When they entered the baptismal waters, they requested to have their right hands raised above the water. They were willing to have all parts of their body baptised, except their right hands that were needed for battle.

Many Christians live like that. They are willing to give certain parts of their lives, but hold back other parts from God. But we must remember the principle spelt out in the 19th century by Hudson Taylor, founder of the China Inland Mission, "Christ is either Lord of all, or is not Lord at all."[46] God wants every part of our life given over to Him, because otherwise we will live in misery. His blood must be applied to every part, and the spiritual medicine must penetrate all aspects of our lives.

To consecrate is to set apart or make holy. What we have been keeping for ourselves must be handed over to Jesus, to be brought under His rule and authority. It involves a surrendering of the heart's throne and the key to the control room of our lives. Dr Thomas Chalmers, the 19th century Scottish preacher, rightly said, "In conversion God gives to me, but in consecration I give to God."[47] We each have to ask ourselves, "Have I returned to God what rightfully belongs to Him?"

The haunting question God asked the ancient Jews, "Will a mere mortal rob God? Yet you rob me" (Malachi 3:8), is a question that extends beyond monetary giving, tithes, and offerings. It is also true when it comes to consecration (how we dedicate ourselves to God's glory). The statement of Paul to the Corinthian Christians—"what I want is not your possessions but you" (2 Corinthians 12:14)—is similar to what God says to us. He does not want parts of our lives but the whole.

In Romans 6, Paul describes the process by which people become slaves to sin. "Do not offer any part of yourself to sin as an instrument of wickedness, but rather offer *yourselves* to God (Romans 6:13, emphasis added).

Note the contrast between the parts and the whole. Satan is masterful at fragmenting our lives into various parts, and then asking just a few of them for himself, the flesh, or the world. But if we give in to this deception, we will soon be like hapless Gulliver who woke up on a beach in Lilliput.[48] The tiny people of Lilliput had worked on the unconscious man, tying down strands of his hair and parts of his clothes to the ground. They worked part by part and succeeded in immobilising him. He had a rude shock when he woke up. He had become their prisoner even though he was stronger and bigger than any one of them.

Is this not how bondage to sin occurs? It is done part by part. However, when God relates with us, it is not bondage but *bonding*. He asks for us to relate to Him wholeheartedly. It is like a marriage where both bride and groom give themselves wholly to each other for the rest of their lives. When we offer the whole, the parts are brought into the bonding as a result (Romans 6:13). If we give the heart to Jesus, then every part of our lives is also given to Him. Like the wise father who tells his son, "My son, give me your heart" (Proverbs 23:26), God speaks to us in the same terms of endearment. He knows that when we give our heart to Jesus, we give everything, as the heart is the centre of our being where intellect, emotions, and will reside. And when we give our hearts to God, He changes our hearts of stone into new hearts that are able to love God (Ezekiel 36:26).

It is possible for a person to go through the motions of piety, attend church and do churchly things, and yet have a heart that is not given to God. Simon the magician who professed to have believed and was baptised in Samaria, nevertheless heard Peter tell him, "your heart is not right before God" (Acts 8:21). He was urged to repent and pray.

It is also possible for a person to have once given his or her heart to Jesus, but over the years taken parts of it back. It may be time to repent and return to Christ what belongs to Him. A key part of giving to God what is owed is letting go of all the things that hold us back from fully trusting and acknowledging Him as Lord of all. The senior years bring with them "a new school of surrender",[49] and we may face new challenges in letting go of things we have been holding on all this time. Paul Tournier notes that "it is only through a series of definitive renunciations that a man becomes aware that he has grown old."[50] What does Tournier mean? Simply this: We progress as we learn to surrender. In his book *A Place for You*, Tournier uses the metaphor of a trapeze artist who can make progress only if he lets go of his current pole to swing and take hold of the next one.[51] We cannot proceed into the future if we hold on to the past. We have to bid farewell to our youthful health, our old careers, and our worldly pursuits.

When we let go, we discover what faith truly is. Imagine life as a series of trapeze poles. When we are able to make good progress by learning how to let go and take hold in turn, when we come to the last pole (which is greased with the finitude of time and human mortality) and finally have to let go, we know we can entrust ourselves to the everlasting and safe hands of God that will catch us (Deuteronomy 33:27). A lifetime of learning trust will help us at the end too. For that to happen, we must learn how to let go and consecrate everything in our lives.

Margaret Magdalen, in her book *A Spiritual Check-Up*, encourages Christians to imagine entering the waters of baptism, and committing each body part, from the feet up to the head, to a life of godly righteousness.[52] Dallas Willard suggests applying this idea in a spiritual exercise:

> I recommend that you then lie on the floor, face down or face up, and explicitly and formally surrender your body to God. Take time to go over the main parts of your body and do the same for each one. What you want to do is to ask God to take charge of your body and each part, to fill it with his life and use it for his purposes.[53]

It is when we surrender every part of our body and every area of our lives to Christ that we become His hands, feet, voice, and ears. This is the "true and proper worship" that Paul writes about as he urges his readers "to offer your bodies as a living sacrifice, holy and pleasing to God" (Romans 12:1). What is true of consecrating and using our physical parts for God's glory is also true of using the other aspects of our lives, such as our time, affections, intellect, relationships, and finances, for the glory of God. These are to be used in obedience to God and for His glory. In this way, we will avoid sinning and becoming distracted or addicted to other things, and live in a focused and meaningful way.

These truths are well expressed in Frances Ridley Havergal's hymn "Take My Life and Let it be", where aspects of one's life (time, hands, feet, voice, finances, intellect, will, heart) are all consecrated to God. The concluding phrase "ever only, all for thee" is a fitting description of such consecration. All this is possible if we trust and obey Christ with all our hearts.

To live a consecrated life is to live a Christ-ruled and Christ-centred life. "Now, who is willing to consecrate themselves to the LORD today" (1 Chronicles 29:5)?

Reflect

- What does it mean to consecrate ourselves to God? How do we do it and what does it involve? What would be the signs of a consecrated life?

- Why do some Christians live un-consecrated lives? How can they find their way to consecrating their hearts and every part to Christ?

Worshipping
Wholeheartedly

American evangelist R. A. Torrey once told this story:
"A young woman in England many years ago always
wore a golden locket that she would not allow anyone to
open or look into, and everyone thought there must be
some romance connected with that locket and that in that
locket must be the picture of the one she loved. The young
woman died at an early age, and after her death the locket
was opened, everyone wondering whose face he would find
within. And in the locket was found simply a little slip of
paper with these words written upon it, "Whom having
not seen, I love." Her Lord Jesus was the only lover she
knew and the only lover she longed for."[54]

Such wholehearted dedication to Christ and love
for God is not common, but is what is required of all

Christians. God's Word repeatedly urges wholehearted love and obedience in our relationship with God.

- "Love the LORD your God with all your heart and with all your soul and with all your strength" (Deuteronomy 6:5; see also Matthew 22:37; Mark 12:30; Luke 10:27).

- "Serve the LORD with all your heart" (1 Samuel 12:20; see also Deuteronomy 10:12; 11:13; Joshua 22:5).

- "You will seek me and find me when you seek me with all your heart" (Jeremiah 29:13; see also Deuteronomy 4:29).

- "I will praise you, LORD, with all my heart" (Psalm 138:1)

- "Give me understanding, so that I may keep your law and obey it with all my heart" (Psalm 119:34)

- "Return to me with all your heart" (Joel 2:12).

- "I, however, followed the LORD my God wholeheartedly" (Joshua 14:8).

- "Serve wholeheartedly, as if you were serving the Lord, not people" (Ephesians 6:7).

These are just a few passages in Scripture that emphasise the importance of relating to God with our whole hearts. It is not possible to follow Christ half-heartedly. After all, Christ said that we must deny ourselves and take up our cross daily if we are to follow Him (Luke 9:23).

Whether we turn to the Lord, and love, obey, and serve Him wholeheartedly will be shown by how we worship God.

God could see through the half-hearted worship of the inhabitants of Israel after its fall to the Assyrians. "Even while these people were worshiping the LORD, they were serving their idols" (2 Kings 17:41). These people were experts in multi-tasking! Even as they worshipped God, they were busy with their idols. Could this be happening today in our churches? How then should we worship God wholeheartedly?

Archbishop William Temple defined worship in a most helpful way. "For worship is the submission of all our nature to God. It is the quickening of *conscience* by His HOLINESS; the nourishment of *mind* with His TRUTH; the purifying of *imagination* by His BEAUTY; the opening of the *heart* to His LOVE; the surrender of *will* to

His PURPOSE—and all of this gathered up in adoration, the most selfless emotion of which our nature is capable and therefore the chief remedy for that self-centeredness which is our original sin and the source of all actual sin."[55]

We must note that worship focuses on God: His holiness, truth, beauty, love, and purpose. In worship, the spotlight falls on God as we behold His nature, character, actions, and will. By nature, we are self-centred people, infected with a stubborn and deadly sinfulness, and addicted to everything else except God. The solution and our only hope is not more of ourselves—our strengths, strategies, achievements, and ambitions. No, our true hope is to turn to God, who alone can save us. This means that our worship services must focus on God, and not on ourselves. He must increase and we must decrease (John 3:30).

Unless our focus in worship is God, we will end up, by default, worshipping ourselves and all that we have made with our hands and minds. But when we truly encounter the living God in worship, we are enabled by the Holy Spirit to submit ourselves to God in every way. Temple's definition shows how the very characteristics of God affect every aspect of our lives. God's holiness turns on and energises our conscience, which is vital for navigating the dubious and ambiguous circumstances in the world.

God's truth feeds our mind. It exposes myths and falsehoods, faulty life goals and assumptions, and helps us to develop the mind of Christ so that we become the people of God's truth. This is necessary if we are to live faithfully in a world of lies and falsehoods. What Satan started at the Garden of Eden continues today— he hoodwinks people with deceitful lies.

It is God's beauty that helps us deal with our polluted imagination. The ancient Israelites were tempted by sinful imagination that sought after idols. They were going after cheap imitations and destroying their souls in the process. True beauty is in God, and it is the beauty of both character and perfection. When we behold God's perfection (His infinity, holiness, power, knowledge, and wisdom) and His incomparable character (His love, mercy, compassion, and faithfulness), we realise how infected our imagination has become. True worship is meeting with God and recognising His beauty, not just by singing "You are beautiful beyond description", but by pondering what that means and letting it cleanse our imagination and make it noble, as God intended for us.

God's love—and what more powerful expression than the cross where God stretched His holy hands to show how much He loves us—touches our heart when we truly glimpse something of its reality in our lives. For true impact, it is necessarily personal. This was the experience of Charles Wesley, who was converted when Scripture touched his heart and he met the Son of God "who loved me and gave himself for me" (Galatians 2:20).[56] It was a personal experience where God's love touched a human heart. This should happen in worship.

True worship seeks the living God as revealed in God's Word and in Christ. When we turn our full attention to Him, His character, and His ways, we will find ourselves changed deeply as God touches every part of who we are. Worship should involve our whole being as we learn to give ourselves wholly to God—that is true worship. Anything less is unacceptable to God and unhelpful to us. As we grow older, we should aspire to worship God in spirit and truth (John 4:24). God is looking for such worshippers, and is pleased when we take time to think about Him, His character and His ways, His beauty and love, and base our worship on these thoughts and reflections. Then our worship will focus on God and arise from the depths of our hearts.

People tend to mellow and grow wiser as they age. They have gathered much from life and can then assess how God has been with them. As they realise that their days on earth are numbered, they have an opportunity to know the difference between what is eternal and what is passing, what is important and what is not. There is a greater likelihood that the importance and centrality of God becomes increasingly and refreshingly clearer. This will make worship much more meaningful and real, and pleasing to the Lord.

Reflect

- Study the passages mentioned about the importance of relating to God wholeheartedly. Reflect on your own journey in the light of your study. Is there something that needs to be done to ensure that you are following Christ wholeheartedly?

- What are some of the distractions in senior years that prevent Christians from loving and serving God wholeheartedly? How can these be overcome?

Finding
Community

We are made for relationships and community, and that is why we all need to belong to a group somewhere. As individuals, we shrivel up when we do not experience an adequate sense of belonging. From the beginning of our lives, we are made to belong to a family, though people have varying experiences of this. Then we belong to a neighbourhood, a school, a workplace, a church, and so on. We need the often "disturbing, upsetting intrusions of others" that "enable them to become agents of God's troubling grace in our pilgrimage." They also become "God's agents of comfort, encouragement and support as we wrestle with the call to come out of the [false] security of our incompleteness into the wholeness God has for us in Christ."[57] We need community to grow into maturity and fullness.

In his old age, the apostle Paul was still writing about his various acquaintances and fellow-workers (2 Timothy 4). He still longed for company, and asked his protégé Timothy to hurry to Rome to meet him, and to bring Mark with him. Some years earlier, Paul wrote to the Romans a letter that was theologically rich, but ended with warm, personal references to various people he knew (Romans 16). There are a number of groups that can be identified in Paul's wide-ranging greetings.

First, there were Paul's *relatives*. We don't know much about Paul's family background. It is likely that he was neither married nor had children of his own. Nevertheless he had relatives. In this letter, he mentions a few of them. He mentions Andronicus and Junias (Romans 16:7 NRSV). They had been converted earlier than Paul, were apostles, and had been in prison with him. They had shared many experiences together, which had undoubtedly strengthened their bonds.

Herodian, another relative, is also mentioned (Romans 16:11 NRSV). Not much is known about this person, but Paul kept in touch and was concerned for him. Later, Paul mentions other relatives in Corinth: Jason and Sosipater (Romans 16:21 NRSV).

Second, Paul mentions his *friends*. Chief among them

were Priscilla and Aquila, a wonderful and respected couple in the early church (Romans 16:3). They had a strong partnership with Paul in his mission to the Gentiles (see Acts 18:2; 1 Corinthians 16:19; 2 Timothy 4:19). They must have spent some time in Rome—but the Emperor Claudius banished the Jews from Rome in AD 52. Paul wrote Romans in about AD 58, so they must have made their way back to Rome by then. Before their return to Rome, Priscilla and Aquila lived in Corinth. They were the couple who first opened their new home to Paul when he arrived there.

This was also the couple Paul went into business with as tent-makers. They later travelled with Paul to Ephesus, where they settled (Acts 18:18–19). Wherever we see Priscilla and Aquila, they have an open home, used for Christian fellowship, worship, teaching, and instruction. This same couple opened their homes to such famous guests as Apollos and instructed him further in his faith (see Acts 18:24–26). They held church meetings in their homes in Corinth, Ephesus, and Rome! Paul expresses his gratitude and fondness. They had risked their lives for him. That's how much they loved one another.

Other fellow-workers were Urbanus (Romans 16:9) and those he mentions as having worked very hard: Mary (v. 6),

Apelles (v. 10), Tryphena, and Tryphosa (v. 12). They were all appreciated by Paul and no doubt shared deep Christian love towards one another. Later, Paul mentions his protégé Timothy (v. 21).

Third, Paul mentions his "dear friends" (the Greek word *agapētos* means beloved, well-loved, or dearly loved). Epenetus (v. 5) was Paul's first convert in Achaia or Asia (depending on manuscripts) and they enjoyed a special relationship. Persis (v. 12) was another dear friend. These were people who knew Paul well. There was obviously a deep friendship between them. Rufus' mother was considered a mother to Paul (v. 13), again reflecting friendship along familial lines. The quality of relationship is best described by Paul when he mentions Ampliatus as "my dear friend in the Lord" (v. 8).

Fourth, there were *others* that Paul considered as having a special relationship with him. He remembers them fondly: Aristobulus (v. 10), Narcissus (v. 11), Rufus (v. 13), and many others in verses 14 and 15. Later, he also mentions Gaius and Erastus in Corinth (v. 23).

All these people had warm, loving relationships with Paul. Many, no doubt, were mentored by him; others, perhaps, were soulmates, and yet others, good friends.

We belong to different groups of people and different

communities. As we age, some of them may become less important, and the bonds between us and them may loosen. For instance, while in school, friendships with classmates are strong, but most will fade into memories later in life, though a few may endure into old age. Some colleagues may also remain part of our lives, even after retirement. There will also be family members, friends, and church members who remain an integral part of our community, even as we grow old. These are important to us, and we must keep connected with them, for their good and ours.

We must also remember that we belong to "the communion of saints" that stretches across time and space. In Christian tradition, we remember those who have gone to be with Jesus, who are part of the "great cloud of witnesses" that cheer us on the way (Hebrews 12:1). As Frederick Buechner points out, we try to understand them, but "through them we come to understand ourselves" too.[58] Advanced in years, we know that we shall soon join them and become part of that wonderful community.

Meanwhile, we should aim to grow old while warm and lovingly connected, not cold and lonely. For this to happen, we must look out for the good of others in our community and give of ourselves to them. We are called to be hospitable and loving in this life. We can touch many groups of people: relatives, friends, colleagues, and others who come into contact with us. This can be done in many ways, depending on our circumstances and health. An active ageing person can meet up regularly with significant others in his life (including family, friends, church members, visitors to church, those they are mentoring). Meeting for a meal, inviting them home, and visiting those who need help and company are some ways this can be done. There are also elder activity centres run by churches where one can enjoy social and spiritual interaction with fellow seniors and volunteers. Seniors can also minister to others through letters, text messages, phone calls, and so on.

Those named or referred to in Paul's list encompass a very broad spectrum. There are men and women, Jews and Gentiles, leaders (see Romans 16:7) and servants, slaves and nobility, and (very likely) rich and poor. Paul died as a man whose life was richly interwoven with his community. It did not happen overnight, but was a sign of a life spent loving, serving, and connecting—and belonging.

Let's be inspired to do the same.

Reflect

· · · · · · · · · ·

- Make a list of communities you are a part of—putting the most significant first. Which of these communities provide you with a strong sense of identity and satisfaction? Why do you think this is the case?

- Is there any community that requires greater attention and involvement on your part? What specific actions can you take to strengthen your bonds with your various communities?

Having a
Ministry Mindset

Many years ago, I was on a Singapore Airlines flight with my wife when an announcement came over the public address system: "Is there a doctor on the flight? We need your help." At that point, I had already stopped practising medicine and my skills were a bit rusty, though I was still registered as a doctor. I hesitated, but when I realised that no one had responded, I spoke to the crew and offered to help. A fellow passenger was feeling sick, and I treated her until she got better. For my efforts, I received a small gift from the airline.

We never know when we will be needed to help someone or provide some kind of ministry. In the story of the Good Samaritan, a wounded man was lying on the road between Jerusalem and Jericho (Luke 10:25–37). A priest and Levite (professional religious workers) were travelling on the same road, saw the man, but passed him by. We are not sure why they did so. Were they in a hurry? Were they afraid that the man who appeared to be a victim was simply a decoy for a group of robbers?

Whatever the case may be, we would expect people connected with religious work to be ready to help victims on the road. But they did not. Perhaps they felt that they had already done their fair share of ministry—in the temple—and were now off-duty. They were like taxi-drivers switching on the "Not For Hire" sign at the end of a long shift. We might also note that they were busy with public ministry (at the temple), but when it came to private ministry they were unwilling to lend a helping hand.

However, the Samaritan, who belonged to a despised race, saw the victim and took pity on him. He stopped and administered first aid. He bandaged the man's wounds and used oil and wine, considered to have medicinal effects in his time. In other words, he was carrying with him, even as he travelled, a kind of first-aid kit, ready to be of service at any time. He was a man who had a ministry mindset. This was further proven in the way he carried the victim to an inn and "took care of him" (Luke 10:34).

At the end of His story, Jesus asked, "Which of these three do you think was a neighbour to the man who fell into the hands of robbers?" (Luke 10:36). The law expert, whose question "And who is my neighbour?" (Luke 10:29) had prompted Jesus to tell the story, replied, "The one who had mercy on him." Jesus told him, "Go and do likewise" (Luke 10:37). The expert did not even want to mention the word "Samaritan" (such was his deep prejudice against them), but he gave the right answer.

Jesus had turned the legal expert's question around. God's Word tells us to love our neighbours (Matthew 22:39; Leviticus 19:18). The right question to ask is not, "Who is my neighbour?" but "What kind of neighbour am I to those around me?"

What makes us a good neighbour to others is our willingness to minister on any occasion, planned and unplanned, and the ability to show mercy and kindness.

The senior years cannot be just a matter of relaxing and reminiscing. It must be about *continuing to serve* by "conforming our lives to the self-giving pattern of Jesus".[59] You may ask, "What can an ageing person like me do in terms of ministry?" You may no longer be in an official position in church, but one does not need to be in some formal leadership or ministry role in order to be a ministering neighbour to others. There are so many ways a senior citizen can be involved in some kind of ministry.

Consider these examples:

- You can pray every Sunday before going to church, asking the Lord to lead you to someone after the service who may need your help. It may just be a word of encouragement, some practical advice, or just a listening ear or comforting prayer that is needed.

- There are younger people in the church who need mentoring, guidance, and encouragement. How about offering some of them your friendship? Talk to them, take them out for a meal, or invite them to your home. Share your spiritual experience with them.

- There are fellow seniors in church who may be struggling with life's many uncertainties. Some may be widowed, others battling chronic or worsening illness, yet others may be homebound and lonely. How about offering your help to them?

- You meet people in the course of daily routines: petrol pump attendants, hawkers, gardeners, and fellow passengers. How about relating with them as a servant of God, ready to attend to any who may need God's help or Word?

Even when an ageing person is homebound, he can still have a ministry mindset. For instance, I read about an elderly lady who realised that she could still play old hymns on her piano. She would call fellow homebound seniors on the phone and play songs for them. Her quiet ministry refreshed so many of her friends.

Whether we have a ministry mindset depends on how we see ourselves. We are children of God and His servants. The aim of life is not to consume or be entertained, but to love and serve. If we remember this, we will see that life is full of opportunities to show mercy and minister to others.

Reflect

- What does having a ministry mindset mean for you? How will it affect your life at home and every time you step outside? What are some factors that make people forget about being good neighbours to others?

- Consider specific things you can do in church and in society that will help you minister to others. Identify specific persons or groups to whom you can offer a listening ear, an encouraging word, or a helping hand.

Part III:

REDEMPTIVE RELATIONSHIPS

Discovering the Heart of Being Human

In his book, *Becoming Human*, Jean Vanier wrote about how "we cannot grow spiritually if we ignore our humanness, just as we cannot become fully human if we ignore spirituality".[60] Though he lived in a different era, John Calvin, the great reformer, said the same thing when he wrote, "Without knowledge of self there is no knowledge of God" and "Without knowledge of God there is no knowledge of self".[61]

Some people have a mistaken idea of Christian maturity; they think it is something that makes us super-spiritual angelic beings. But that is not what the Bible says. Being saved in Christ and being made holy actually makes us true human beings. I am defining "true human being" as the state God first created us to be in—perfect and in perfect union with Him. That was God's intention for humans, how He wanted us to be. But we lost this humanness in the Garden of Eden, when God's image in us became marred.

We were all created in the image of God (Genesis 1:27), but that image has been lost because of our sins. The heart of the human race has become deceitful (Jeremiah 17:9). Then Jesus, the Son of God, became a man. He was the only truly human being who lived on earth, as God intended human beings to live. He shared in our humanity (and remained sinless), "fully human in every way", so that by His death we may be saved (Hebrews 2:14–18). When we believe in Jesus and walk as He did (1 John 2:6), then we shall become like Him, "being transformed into his image" (2 Corinthians 3:18). In this way, the image of God is restored in us and we become truly human, as God originally intended us to be. This is God's purpose for saving us (Romans 8:29).

Those who follow Jesus learn to become truly human. How do we understand this? We are born into a sinful, noisy, crowded, and competitive world. In this Darwinian jungle, we learn quickly, in the words of Darwinian atheist Richard Dawkins, to be "survival machines",[62] and in so doing, we become less than human—sub-human. We become members of the rat race, competing for advantageous positions (whether it is wealth, power, position, or influence) as we fight for territory, space, and worldly success.

If this is our view of life, then we might agree with the British philosopher Thomas Hobbes who described the natural state of life as "solitary, poor, nasty, brutish, and short".[63] He therefore argued for society to be organised such that life could become more civilised. But even in our most organised societies, we find selfishness, meanness, violence, and crime. Can we become more human—more of what God intended us to be—simply by organising ourselves, or through education and better healthcare?

Further reflection will lead us to the conclusion that no amount of civilising actions can alter the sub-human reality in us. We may dress up nicely and relate to each other with courtesy, but in our private and unguarded moments, ugliness will still rear its head. Even the most civilised of groups can transform into a violent mob when exposed to stressful situations or deceptive slogans. The sight of hundreds of thousands mesmerised by a madman such as Hitler, or scores of American young men fighting in Vietnam and degenerating into cruel killing machines, as seen in the infamous My Lai massacre of 1968, are examples of this.

What then is the real solution to the sub-human reality deep within us—also known as our inherent sinfulness? God is the only real solution, for only He has the power to recreate, reform, and renew us into real human beings.

There are many ways we can look at this. The spiritual writer Henri Nouwen, in his book *Reaching Out*, spells out three movements that must take place in our lives if we are to find our true selves.[64]

We must first move *from illusion to God*. We carry in our hearts illusions of God—we can call them idols. Many man-made deities, both ancient and modern, are reflections of our fallen selves. But when we come to Christ, we see a God who defies our fallen ideas. How can a God who created the universe die on the cross for us? When we see the cross, we see a God who loves us perfectly and deeply, and will go to any length to save us from our sins, delusions, and illusions. The more we see of this true God, the more human we can become. This is also seen in two other significant movements.

First, the movement *from loneliness to solitude*. Human life, in its most painful form, is a lonely experience. But when we find God, we find our God-given space. We realise that under God's sovereign and loving rule, we each have a space generously given by the God who loves us. As Augustine famously said so long ago, we will be restless until we find our rest in God.[65] When we find God and our true human space, we can rest and be restored. There is no more need to impress others and ourselves, to compete for a space that is already ours.

Spiritual director Kathleen Fischer notes, "At its deepest level all loneliness reflects our common experience that no created goods fully answer our yearnings; loneliness is rooted in a longing for God. It becomes solitude when the voice of God is heard in its stillness."[66]

Second, because we have our God-given space, we can then give others their space. We move *from hostility to hospitality*, and thus become more human, because we are created for nurturing relationships, to be friends rather than enemies. When we discover Christ and His love, we can give up our pretensions and masks, our survival tactics and self-centredness. We can then develop the true face of a human being, and learn to be more loving, joyful, peaceful, humble, gentle, forgiving, patient, self-controlled, good, and kind.

In our old age, we may carry scars from frequent skirmishes in the Darwinian world of self-centred one-upmanship and extreme consumption and greed. But as we age, there is a priceless opportunity to give up old habits and worldviews and be truly converted. We must turn to Christ and become truly human. We must discover that "our lives are gifts, not achievements".[67] Pastor and writer Charles Swindoll reminds us, "Please don't forget—God has decided to let you live this long. Your old age is not a mistake . . . nor an oversight . . . nor an afterthought."[68] Old age provides an opportunity to realise that there is much to thank God for, that He loves us, and that our life is His gracious gift. To realise these things helps us become more human—as God intended us to be.

Reflect

- Do you agree that much of life in this world turns us into less than human? What evidence can you think of to support or refute this idea?

- Why do you think that coming to Christ (and staying with Him) is a real opportunity for us to become truly human? What would constitute this process of being and becoming human? What would be at its heart? Assess your own life in the light of your reflections.

18

Friendship

An old man once prayed, "Grant me the senility to forget the people I never liked anyway, the good fortune to run into the ones I do, and the eyesight to tell the difference."[69]

In old age, we may or may not remember meeting so many people; some were passing acquaintances, others lingered in our lives longer. Among the latter there would be some we never really got to know and even some we decidedly did not want to know. But there would be a few who have become our true friends.

How do such friendships develop? Friendship has been written about in classical Christian literature, by authors such as Augustine, Thomas Aquinas, Aelred of Rievaulx, and Francis de Sales.[70] They all agree that for healthy and deep friendships to develop, there needs to be:

- Equality: Human friends need to be on equal terms, and treat each other with dignity and mutual respect.

- Goodwill: The Greek philosopher Aristotle and others have described false friendships as those sought for personal advantage. True friendships are motivated by goodwill.

- Mutual disclosure: For this to happen, there needs to be mutual trust. Twelfth century English monk Aelred of Rievaulx writes about the trust and goodwill between true friends: "One confides everything to a true friend as if he were his other self".[71]

In everyday conversations, people are generally superficial and task-oriented. Even among friends, conversations can focus more on information than on what weighs on the heart, on facts rather than feelings.

One of the greatest gifts we can give in friendship is that of active listening. Active listening is attentive listening that focuses on feelings. Pity has to do with feeling *about* the other person; the focus is still on ourselves. Sympathy is better and has to do with feeling *with* the other person, but we may get entangled with the person's problems and drown in their sorrow. Empathy is the best response, for it has to do with feeling *into* a person, and we are then able to respond compassionately. When communication involves feelings and when pronouns such as "I", "you", and "we" are used, it means we are communicating with one another deeply.

We must be careful to guard against obstacles that short-circuit the process of active listening and the development of friendship. They are: prejudice, preoccupation, defensiveness, fear, lack of compassion, and so on. The more we overcome these barriers, the more we can become friends.

As we age, we must also be aware of the seasons of a friendship. Paula Ripple discusses the spring, summer, fall, and winter of friendships.[72] *Spring* is a season of excitement and discovery. New friendships are easier to sustain because there has been no time of testing, no past memory of coldness or conflict (see Song of Songs 2:10–12).

Summer is the season of growth, inner security, and surer communication (see Philippians 1:3, 6–7). *Fall* is marked by the profound loneliness that is experienced even in friendship. We come to terms with our own loneliness, a part of life no friend or lover can take away from us. There is a need to discover personal solitude (see John 14:1–2, 4).

Winter is the season that brings out the faithfulness of friendship: the faithfulness to commitments and the quiet celebration of a long friendship (see Proverbs 17:17). This tells us that friendship is a journey and can mature over time; it has its various seasons and challenges.

As we age, we need to reflect on our friendships with significant others. We have to ask questions and reflect on our active listening: Who are the people I like to listen to? Who are the people who are difficult for me to listen to? Who listens to me when it is important? When did my listening help someone? When did I fail to listen to someone who needed me? When did someone fail to listen to me? How do I listen?

We can learn much from Jesus, who told His disciples, "I have called you friends, for everything that I learned from my Father I have made known to you" (John 15:15). He also said, "Greater love has no one than this: to lay down one's life for one's friends" (John 15:13). The marks of true friendship are sacrificial love and trusting transparency.

Our friendship with Jesus helps us to be true friends to others. Can you think of some old and new friends who need your friendship?

Reflect

- A famous friendship in the Bible is that of David and Jonathan. Read 1 Samuel 18:1; 19:1–7; 20:1–42; 2 Samuel 1:25–26; 9:1–12. How would you characterise their friendship? Are there implications for any of your friendships?

- Make a list of friends you have under the four seasons of friendship discussed in this chapter. How do you keep in touch with old close friends? Are you developing new friendships? Ask yourself what sort of friend you are to others.

Engaging and
Enjoying the Family

Family life is one of life's highest blessings, especially if one is blessed with a loving and caring family. Some of the best memories a person can have are related to his family: growing up, falling in love, getting married, having children, and experiencing significant family moments of pain and suffering, crisis and challenge, as well as joy and laughter.[73]

But for some, family life can also be the place where the greatest hurts are experienced. Some may recall little more than unfaithfulness, neglect, abuse, and strained relationships when they think of their families. As family relationships are often the closest social relationships we have, they make us most vulnerable. Family members have the greatest potential to inflict pain.

How a family functions or malfunctions can become a pattern that is repeated down the generations. The biblical stories of the ancient patriarchs demonstrate this. Take, for instance, Abraham's response to personal danger. God had called him to leave Ur to go to Canaan. When there was a famine in Canaan, Abraham decided to go to Egypt to survive. Before entering Egypt, he told his wife, Sarai, "I know what a beautiful woman you are. When the Egyptians see you, they will say, 'This is his wife.' Then they will kill me but will let you live. Say you are my sister, so that I will be treated well for your sake and my life will be spared because of you" (Genesis 12:11–13).

Notice immediately Abraham's strategy of self-preservation. He lied to save his own skin. Worse, he was willing to sacrifice his wife's safety and honour for his own survival. In that panicky moment of fear for his life, he ignored all that God had promised him—that he and his wife would produce a great nation (Genesis 12:2).

Years later, Abraham's son Isaac went to the land of the Philistines to escape another famine. There, he repeated his father's mistake (Genesis 26:1–11). Fearing for his life, he lied that his wife Rebekah was his sister.

The two stories bear a striking resemblance. It was as if the very same script had been handed down from one generation to the next. Other scripts are also played out in this ancient family. For example, the story of favouritism. Isaac favoured his son Esau (Genesis 25:28). Esau's twin brother Jacob plotted with his mother (who favoured him) to deceive his father, who was blind because of old age. He managed to divert Isaac's intended blessing for Esau to himself. Years later, Jacob similarly favoured his son Joseph above all the other siblings (Genesis 37:3).

How do such family "scripts" get passed on? The usual answers are nature (genes), nurture (upbringing), and spirit (spiritual heritage or baggage). Though this is not the place to discuss them in detail, probably all three are true.

The more important thing is determining what to do with our family scripts. If they are good, we must pass on the blessings. If they are bad, we must write new scripts to replace them. Whatever the case, we must discover the story of Jesus, whose script is found in Scripture. When we place our faith in Christ and walk with Him, we can live out His script, which involves love, forgiveness, righteousness, and faithfulness.

We are never too old to do something positive about our family lives. Perhaps some elderly people feel a sense of regret at having messed up. But as long as we are alive, we can bless our families. Here are some thoughts:

- Confess the things you have done against your family members and ask them for forgiveness. Likewise, be willing to forgive those who have hurt you in the past. It is good to end our earthly lives with a sense of closure as we follow Jesus who, before He died, prayed for His enemies and tormentors to be forgiven (Luke 23:34).

- You may have more time in your senior years to devote to family members, offering a listening ear and a sympathetic helping hand.

- If you have grandchildren, you can pass on your family's good heritage by investing in their lives. Some grandparents act as foster parents to their grandchildren because the parents are too busy and stressed out with their daily routines. But some become resentful at having to carry such a burden in old age, especially if they are not appreciated. Some heart-to-heart sharing and negotiation may help.

- Pray for your family members daily, bringing them into God's light where they can receive His promises and loving attention.

• Remember that family relationships are not meant to hurt, but to heal. We are not meant to hate but to love, not to hide but to know and be known, not to blame but to forgive.[74] If you have not done this before, take a family picture, and by faith, see Jesus in that picture. What a difference that makes!

• As a grandparent or an ageing parent, you can leave your family what is ultimately valuable and important to you. Don't leave behind merely superficial trinkets of life (material things and passing fancies), but the very spiritual treasures that you have found.

Christian writer and poet John Leax put it well when writing about his grandfather:[75]

Spilled from a mildewed box
  you are
  the pieces of a faded puzzle
  working alone I have spread your dull colors
  face up on the table
  but have done no more
  you are
  difficult
  I have tried all the combinations

but failed to build even your border
for you have given me extra pieces
and withheld the one I need

How important it is to remember that "Grandchildren are the crown of the aged" (Proverbs 17:6 ESV). What does the above poem mean? Simply this: The one thing we often withhold from our family members, for various reasons, is our heart. We need to turn our hearts towards our loved ones. Consider the intergenerational biblical portrait of old people in the same scene as children playing. "Once again old men and women will walk Jerusalem's streets with their canes and will sit together in the city squares. And the streets of the city will be filled with boys and girls at play" (Zechariah 8:4–5 NLT). What a wonderful picture!

Reflect

- How can family life be both a blessing and a crucible of pain and suffering? Why do the closest relationships have the potential to do the most damage? How can this be avoided?

- Take time to write down a list of your family members (both immediate and extended). For each, write down where you think they are in their life journeys, and what their aspirations, anxieties, and needs are. Assess your relationship with each and determine how you can minister to them as a senior member of the family.

Mentoring the
Next Generation

The concept of mentoring is something that is being explored in many circles. Basically, mentoring means getting alongside someone to bring out the best in him by giving advice based on our own experience.

The concept of mentoring can be found in Scripture. In the Old Testament, parents are expected to be spiritual mentors to their children. "Impress them on your children. Talk about them when you sit at home and when you walk along the road, when you lie down and when you get up. Tie them as symbols on your hands and bind them on your foreheads. Write them on the door-frames of your houses and on your gates" (Deuteronomy 6:7–9).

What is true for biological parents is also true for spiritual ones. The apostle Paul refers to himself and his team of God's servants as spiritual parents. "Just as a nursing mother cares for her children, so we cared for you. Because we loved you so much, we were delighted to share with you not only the gospel of God but our lives as well . . . For you know that we dealt with each of you as a father deals with his own children, encouraging, comforting and urging you to live lives worthy of God, who calls you into his kingdom and glory" (1 Thessalonians 2:7–8, 11–12).

Life is not just to be lived for ourselves, but for others, and living for others involves not just Christian service, but also mentoring the next generation. Older Christians have an important responsibility to mentor younger ones, especially in their local churches. Are we doing it? I suspect that very little of this is going on. There may be occasional conversations about spiritual matters, but even this is often missing in interaction between the old and young.

Perhaps seniors may say that they were never mentored themselves; thus they find it difficult to mentor others due to a lack of experience. They may have attended classes or seminars on spiritual growth, but that is not quite the same as mentoring, which is often a one-to-one, intentional process, and very personal in nature.

But even though a senior may not have been mentored before, he or she can still learn to do it for two reasons.

Firstly, we are all called to be apprenticed to Jesus, who invites us to learn from Him. He opens Scripture to us (see Luke 24:13–35) and walks with us. Through His Spirit, He guides and disciples us. So, in one sense, we cannot say that we have not been mentored before, if we are followers of Christ.

Second, we can study Scripture and learn from good examples of mentoring, like how Jesus trained His disciples, and how people like Paul mentored younger men like Timothy and Titus.[76] We can also read the many books that have been written on mentoring.[77]

Referring to the special mentoring relationship he had with the younger Timothy, Paul wrote, "You, however, know all about my teaching, my way of life, my purpose, faith, patience, love, endurance, persecutions, sufferings" (2 Timothy 3:10–11). Paul's life was like an open book to Timothy, who learned from Paul's instruction and example in various key aspects of life. Notice the broad range of Paul's list. These things are best learned in the school of life, as an apprenticeship.

We should remember Swiss physician Paul Tournier's advice: "Success in retirement depends in great measure on the way we lived beforehand."[78] Indeed, how we live in retirement draws a lot on how we have lived before. This is true not only for our personal growth but also for how we nurture and influence others. There are five key actions that can bring a mentoring relationship forward:

- **See the potential of a mentee.** Paul noted Timothy's heritage, calling, and giftedness (2 Timothy 1:3–7), and invested his time and effort in Timothy's life.

- **Encourage the mentee to guard his gifts.** Paul indicates that Timothy must "guard the good deposit that was entrusted" to him (2 Timothy 1:14). In 2 Timothy 2:1–7, we find Paul giving clear instructions to his protégé on how he can invest his special giftedness. Specifically, Paul uses three analogies to convey this message on guarding. Paul knows that if Timothy was to fulfil his life's passion, he must learn to think from the perspectives of a soldier, athlete, and farmer.

- **Warn the mentee of potential weaknesses.** In 2 Timothy 2:20–23, Paul broadly mentions areas that will strengthen Timothy's life and ministry and others that will weaken and undermine him.

- **Emphasise perseverance.** Paul realistically indicates the scope of difficulties that Timothy would have to face in 2 Timothy 3:1–9.

- **Be an example.** Paul boldly declares that Timothy should follow his example when investing his life, so that he would not be disappointed (2 Timothy 3:14). We are called to the "ministry of example".[79]

Older Christians have an important responsibility to nurture younger Christians through mentoring relationships. We need to ask, "Do I have my 'Timothys'? If not, can I spot any?" If we can pass on our blessings to those we leave behind, we may end our life like Abraham, who "died at a ripe old age, old and contented" (Genesis 25:8 HCSB).[80] That is a good way to live, and a good way to die.

Reflect

. . . .

• Think of those who have been a "Paul" in your life, mentoring and encouraging you in the past. What did you learn from them? Think also of those who are your "Timothys" or who could be such. What concrete steps can you take to initiate or continue these mentoring relationships?

• Read 2 Timothy 3:10–11. Reflect on the various aspects of Paul's legacy in terms of teaching, way of life, purpose, faith, patience, endurance, and sufferings. Discuss what should be the core teachings we should leave behind among our family, friends, colleagues, and mentees.

Redemptive Conversations

Some researchers claim that, on average, men speak about 7,000 words daily while women speak 20,000 words; others say that both genders speak about 16,000 words.[81] That is a lot of words, and considering what Jesus said about being careful with our words, we should reflect deeply. Jesus warned, "I tell you, on the day of judgement people will give account for every careless word they speak, for by your words you will be justified, and by your words you will be condemned" (Matthew 12:36–37 ESV). It seems that all the words we have spoken will come back to haunt us.

The apostle James points out that the tongue is resistant to our attempts to tame it and is probably the last part of the body to be brought under control (James 3:3–12). It boasts, tells lies, curses others, and is "a restless evil, full of deadly poison" (James 3:8). We need to practise the proper custody of the tongue if we are to honour God and bless others. An Egyptian desert father (in the early centuries of the church) said, "It is impossible to advance in virtue without custody of the tongue."[82]

Every word that comes forth from God's mouth gives us life and sustains us (Matthew 4:4). As we continue to walk with Christ, and as we age in years, should not our speech reflect the gracious and life-sustaining speech of God? The book of Proverbs gives much wisdom on doing this:

- "Those who guard their mouths and their tongues keep themselves from calamity" (21:23).

- "The mouth of the righteous is a fountain of life" (10:11).

- "The tongue of the righteous is choice silver . . . The lips of the righteous nourish many" (10:20–21).

- "Like apples of gold in settings of silver is a word spoken in right circumstances" (25:11 NASB).

- "A person finds joy in giving an apt reply—and how good is a timely word!" (15:23).

As part of being made holy, our speech will change. Paul urges us, "Let your conversation be always full of grace, seasoned with salt, so that you may know how to answer everyone" (Colossians 4:6).

We will have many conversations with family members, neighbours, friends, church members, and strangers. How can we carry on a conversation that is good, life-giving, and redemptive? The Lord Jesus set the example. We read in John 4 about an extended conversation between Him and a Samaritan woman (John 4:7–26). We can learn many lessons from it.

First, the conversation was *deep*. Jesus began by expressing a need—He was thirsty and requested water. That led to a discussion on thirst and water, and the Lord used the opportunity to introduce the water that quenches spiritual thirst. The woman then asked a theological question about the location of true worship. Jesus made some quick comments and then moved on to talk about the kind of worshippers that the Father is seeking.

Second, the conversation was *personal*. Jesus encouraged the woman to reveal her true self—she was living in sin and shame. Realising that Jesus somehow knew all about her, she disclosed her true self to Him. He then showed that her theological question hid a personal problem: she was unable to worship God in her heart because of her sin and shame. If God cannot be worshipped in her heart, it does not matter where she goes to worship God; she will not be able to do so. Jesus also revealed His true identity to her.

Third, the conversation was *redemptive*. The woman came as a sinner, wrapped up in shame; she had avoided the people of her town by going to the well alone at noon. But after Jesus gently led her to the truth about himself, she finally realised and accepted who He was. In quick succession, as the truth gradually dawned on her, she addressed Jesus as "Jew", "Sir", "Prophet", and finally "Messiah". What a splendid discovery! And what a redemptive conversation! Healed and transformed, she hurried into the town and told the people whom she was earlier too ashamed to meet that the Messiah was nearby, and brought them to Him.

We have many opportunities today to hold redemptive conversations, Jesus-style. Seniors possess the life experience and maturity to make a difference in many conversations. We need to make our conversations deep, personal, and redemptive, by treating others as individuals with needs. Beyond discussing current issues and events (important in their own right), we can dive deeper into spiritual matters by addressing personal concerns and needs. Behind what others say intellectually or pragmatically lie spiritual needs and questions, struggles and aspirations. If we listen closely, we can make our conversations redemptive.

Ageing people can speak with wisdom, like Christian sages, and offer encouraging and healing words. In the ancient Benedictine monastic tradition, each day begins with a prayer: "Dear Lord, please help me today to use my tongue in your service by uttering words of love, kindness, praise, and encouragement. Help me to take custody of my tongue so I do not utter words of hate, disrespect, criticism, gossip, or slander."

We can pray likewise.

Reflect
....

- Why is it important to watch our words every day? How would you assess the words you speak? How much of them are positive and how much are negative? Is there any adjustment needed in how you speak to others, both in *what* you say and *how* you say it?

- Reflect on the way Jesus conducted a redemptive conversation. What personal lessons are there for you? How can you make your conversations deeper, more personal, and more redemptive?

Praying for Others

Christian apologist Lee Strobel tells this amazing true story:

> In Equatorial Africa, far from pharmacies and hospitals, a woman died in childbirth, leaving behind a grieving two-year-old daughter and a premature baby in danger of succumbing to the chill of the night. With no incubator, no electricity, and few supplies, the newborn's life was in jeopardy.
>
> A helper filled a hot water bottle to maintain the warmth desperately needed by the infant, but suddenly the rubber burst—and it was the last hot water bottle in the village.
>
> A visiting missionary physician from Northern Ireland, Dr Helen Roseveare, asked the orphans to pray for the

situation—but a faith-filled ten-year-old named Ruth seemed to go too far.

"Please, God, send us a water bottle," she implored. "It'll be no good tomorrow, God, the baby'll be dead; so please send it this afternoon." As if that request was not sufficiently audacious, she added, "And while You are about it, would You please send a dolly for the little girl so she'll know You really love her?"

A couple of hours later, a car dropped off a twenty-two-pound package. The orphans helped open it and sort through the contents: some clothing for them, bandages for the leprosy patients, and a bit of food.

Oh, and this: "As I put my hand in again, I felt the . . . could it really be? I grasped it, and pulled it out. Yes. A brand-new rubber, hot water bottle!" said Roseveare. "I cried. I had not asked God to send it; I had not truly believed that He could."

With that, little Ruth rushed forward. "If God has sent the bottle, He must have sent the dolly too!" she exclaimed.

She dug through the packaging and found it at the bottom of the parcel: a beautifully dressed doll. Asked

Ruth, "Can I go over with you, Mummy, and give this dolly to that little girl, so she'll know that Jesus really loves her?"

That parcel had been packed five months earlier by Roseveare's former Sunday school class. The leader, feeling prompted by God, included the hot water bottle; a girl contributed the doll.

And this package, the only one ever to arrive, was delivered the same day Ruth prayed for it with the faith of a child.[83]

This story warms our heart, reminding us of how God operates in our world in amazing ways. It also tells us of the power of intercessory prayer, when we learn to pray for others.

We naturally pray for others, especially when they are facing crisis or have some needs. And God does answer such prayers. But not many pray regularly for others, apart from possibly family members. The Bible encourages us to pray for:

- Fellow Christians (Ephesians 6:18)

- Pastors, missionaries, and other servants of God (1 Thessalonians 5:25)

- The sick (James 5:14–16)

- Those in authority (1 Timothy 2:1–2)

- Enemies and persecutors (Matthew 5:44)

We can use several intercessory prayers as models. For instance, the apostle Paul prayed for fellow Christians in Philippians 1:9–11; Ephesians 1:17–19; 3:14–19; Colossians 1:9–12. We can substitute the names of others and pray for them using the same words.

We can also think about where in their journey with God different people are, what their needs may be, and pray accordingly. When people ask us to pray for them, we should not only say that we will, but actually do it!

We can pray for those we will be meeting on a particular day, or those we meet incidentally. We need to pray for those struggling with sickness and hospitalisation—and pray with a regularity that will not only enable us to bring them daily before God's throne, but also remind us of their needs and perhaps reveal how we can be of service to them and their loved ones.

There are so many people we know who have needs—in our families, among our friends, in church, in our workplace, and in our neighbourhood. How wonderful it would be if we brought them all to God in prayer!

We can even pray for those we read about in the media—victims of tragedy, people who are serving others and doing good, individuals trapped in crime, and many more.

Older folks may have more time available to pray unhurriedly, bringing people before God. It is a great ministry that not only glorifies God and helps others, but also builds our spiritual lives. We may lose physical strength and stamina, and even our mobility, but we can always pray, even on hospital beds and wheelchairs. It is the spiritual discipline we can hold on to right to the end.

In praying for others, we learn to be like Jesus who, even now, is at the right hand of the Father interceding for us (Romans 8:34; Hebrews 7:25). Jesus, along with the Holy Spirit (Romans 8:27), is the Divine Intercessor. When we pray for others, we join the Lord and His Spirit in praying to the Father. Isn't that amazing? We are caught up with the internal intercession that is going on within the Trinity. What a great mystery and privilege![84]

Reflect

- Why is intercessory prayer a necessary part of Christian discipleship? See chapter for a list of people we ought to pray for. See also Luke 11:9; Colossians 4:2; Romans 12:12; 1 Thessalonians 5:16–18. Make a list of people you ought to be praying for. What do you think you should be asking God for on their behalf? Turn your thoughts to actual prayer, and do it regularly. Learn to use the intercessory prayers in the Bible to pray for others.

- What do you think Jesus is interceding for you about before the Father? How about for those you know? Ask God to show you how to pray for others, and pray accordingly. Why do you think such prayer leads to loving actions?

Part IV:

HEALTH AND FRAILTIES

Staying Healthy

The original "Methodists" were a group of Greek physicians in the first century who prescribed an effective method for gaining good health: a proper diet and regular exercise.

It appears that these ancient physicians discovered something that remains true even now. In most advice about good health, these two points are often emphasised: watch what you eat and get some regular exercise. And this is sound advice.

This method of remaining in good health is still relevant, especially for those advancing in years. It can reduce the chance of developing chronic illnesses such as diabetes and hypertension, and slow down physical and mental deterioration associated with old age.

Many seniors take their health quite seriously, what with loads of advice available on the internet and newspapers, and countless WhatsApp messages received from well-meaning friends and family members. They take health supplements (a multi-billion dollar industry), try the latest fads, and attempt to remain healthy and strong for as long as is possible.

Some seniors may become obsessed with physical health.[85] They spend an inordinate amount of time and money religiously guarding their health. In the process, they end up pursuing good physical health rather than God and His righteousness. When an ageing senior gets up without fail every morning to go for a jog or brisk walk, but does not practise regular Bible reading and prayer, he is getting his priorities wrong. Paul, as a veteran missionary, advised his protégé Timothy to drink a little wine for his stomach condition and frequent illnesses (1 Timothy 5:23). In addition, he wrote, "Physical exercise has some value, but spiritual exercise is valuable in every way, because it promises life both for the present and for the future" (1 Timothy 4:8 GNT).

Physical exercise has its proper place, but it should not replace spiritual exercise. The pursuit of physical health is good but must always be done in the context of pursuing spiritual health and well-being. We must remember that "Grey hair is a crown of splendour; it is attained in the way of righteousness" (Proverbs 16:31).

There is a danger that lying at the heart of the modern obsession with physical health is an unhealthy desire to avoid, consciously and unconsciously, the ultimate death that awaits all human beings. Are we willing to lose physical health in the pursuit of God's glory? Or, if we are already in relatively poor health, are we willing to serve God well?

Many faithful servants of God served the Lord in relatively poor health. Paul had to live and serve with his "thorn in my flesh" (generally understood to be a painful chronic physical condition) even though he prayed three times for the ailment to be removed from his body (2 Corinthians 12:7–9). According to tradition, Paul also suffered from bow legs, perhaps as a result of his frequent beatings and injuries (see 2 Corinthians 11:23–27). These did not prevent him from faithfully fulfilling God's calling.

The leaders of the Reformation suffered from many illnesses and frailties. Martin Luther had a long list of troubles: piles, constipation, cataracts, fainting spells, arthritis, kidney and bladder stones, and chest pains. John Calvin was physically frail and suffered from consumption (tuberculosis), ulcerated haemorrhoids, gout, kidney stones, and other distressing ailments. He was very careful with his diet because of stomach troubles and ate only one meal a day. He died at the age of 55, having had a prolific writing ministry and having served as the pastor of Geneva and a leading reformer.

Charles Spurgeon, the prince of preachers, suffered from debilitating gout, arthritis, kidney disease, and depression, and yet he worked 18 hours a day, preparing sermons, writing tracts, counselling, and lecturing. He had a view about suffering and hard work that would not sit well with today's obsession with physical health and personal well-being. He wrote:

> If by excessive labour, we die before reaching the average age of man, worn out in the Master's service, then glory be to God, we shall have so much less of earth and so much more of Heaven![86]

Modern sentiments may be expressed better as "Stay healthy to stay useful". But the point is that the pursuit of health should not become an idol at the expense of our pursuit of God and His glory. We must apply common sense by watching our diet and getting regular exercise (walking is a good exercise for seniors). But we must be prepared to stretch ourselves in self-giving love and serve God even in poor health. We must seek Him and His righteousness—that should always be first above other concerns and pursuits (Matthew 6:33).

Reflect

- Why is it important to remain in good health? Think of how you are doing this and what more you can do. What are the limitations of pursuing good health?

- What can you learn from those who suffer chronic ailments and yet have a positive perspective of life and ministry? How can you ensure that your pursuit of God remains top priority?

Coming to Terms with Declining Health

Old age, according to Christian writer Helen Oppenheimer, is characterised by both fruition and decay, fulfilment and loss.[87] Or, we may say that old age is both a special gift and a special burden.[88] The writer of the deeply philosophical book Ecclesiastes describes old age realistically, to the extent that it may make an ageing person despair:

> *Honor and enjoy your Creator while you're still young,*
> *Before the years take their toll and your vigor wanes,*
> *Before your vision dims and the world blurs*
> *And the winter years keep you close to the fire.*
>
> *In old age, your body no longer serves you so well.*
> *Muscles slacken, grip weakens, joints stiffen.*
> *The shades are pulled down on the world.*
> *You can't come and go at will. Things grind to a halt.*

The hum of the household fades away.
You are wakened now by bird-song.
Hikes to the mountains are a thing of the past.
Even a stroll down the road has its terrors.
Your hair turns apple-blossom white,
Adorning a fragile and impotent matchstick body.
Yes, you're well on your way to eternal rest,
While your friends make plans for your funeral.
(Ecclesiastes 12:1–5 The Message)

This is a portrayal of an ageing body that is breaking down. Old age brings with it failing eyesight, decreasing energy, strength, and flexibility, loss of hearing and teeth, and sleeplessness. The body loses its beauty, leaving behind scars and other ravages of time. The systems in the body begin to crumble.

Some people find it difficult to accept this, and try their best to deny it by pretending to remain youthful, at least in appearance and lifestyle—thus repudiating the true honour of old age.[89] An awareness that one is ageing can lead to both hyperactivity (increased activities) or hypo-activity (too much slowing down).[90] In our age-denying culture, the former is the bigger phenomenon. But you can't fight ageing for long. Degeneration eventually wins.

The apostle Paul states the hard facts: "outwardly we are wasting away" (2 Corinthians 4:16). Elsewhere, in deep theological reflection, he observes that creation is "subjected to frustration" and in "bondage to decay" (Romans 8:20–21). In our present universe, because of sin and its consequences, everything is set to decay (the more scientifically inclined of us may remember the Second Law of Thermodynamics). This includes the breaking down of our body and its proper functioning. Those who are suffering from the effects of ageing know this from personal experience.

According to Paul, we "groan inwardly as we wait eagerly for our adoption to sonship, the redemption of our bodies" (Romans 8:23). Note that amid crumbling bodies, we look forward to our redemption, including that of our bodies. There is hope, but we must accept the present reality of declining health and failing bodies—that will lead to death.

Ageing can bring with it many anxieties. There is the fear of pain and of failing to cope with life's normal duties and routines. What if a stroke occurs and one becomes bedridden or wheelchair bound? How would one cope with the loss of freedom, mobility, and independence? What about rising medical costs; how can one afford increasingly frequent treatment? Will one become redundant, a burden to others? American governor of Colorado Richard Lamm once said, rather alarmingly, that terminally ill elderly people have a "duty to die and get out of the way"![91] Would one be discarded as a heavy burden on society?

Doctors say that the last 10 years of a person's life are typically very difficult, as health fails and increasingly frequent and urgent medical attention is needed.[92] People worry about how life will end for them. What will they have to face?

How can one prepare for this deterioration in health?[93] Psalm 71 is comforting for ageing people. It echoes the feelings of growing old: "Do not cast me away when I am old; do not forsake me when my strength is gone" (v. 9). There is an awareness that natural strength is failing, and a fear that one may be forsaken and forgotten by God. But a growing relationship with God—knowing, trusting, and obeying God—makes this prayer poignant and hopeful. "Since my youth, God, you have taught me" (v. 17).

The ageing person in Psalm 71 is full of hope in God. "Though you have made me see troubles, many and bitter, you will restore my life again; from the depths of the earth you will again bring me up" (v. 20). God will rescue us from pain and death, and be with us in our time of need.

Because of his hope and prayer, the ageing person is able to make the best use of the remaining years, declaring

God's power to the next generation (v. 18). "All day long", he or she will be speaking of God's goodness and righteousness (vv. 15, 24), even amid the pain, weakness, and uncertainty of old age.

The frailties of old age may actually be a hidden blessing. In the mid-19th century, William Mountford wrote these words:

> Is your eyesight dimmer? Then the world is seen by you in cathedral light. Is your hearing duller? Then it is just as though you were always where loud voices and footsteps ought not to be heard . . . Yes, for twilight and silence . . . old age makes us like daily dwellers in the house of the Lord.[94]

Indeed, the increasing frailty an ageing person experiences may actually serve to heighten his awareness of a reality and life beyond our normal senses. An older person whose physical senses are declining, and yet displays increasing joy and contentment, would be a great encouragement to others. Younger ones will be inspired. God will be glorified. We will say with the psalmist, "My flesh and my heart may fail, but God is the strength of my heart and my portion forever" (Psalm 73:26).

Reflect

· · · · · · · · · ·

- Reflect on Ecclesiastes 12:1–5. What feelings does the passage evoke in you? Why do you think this is so? Share with fellow seniors your thoughts and concerns and discuss what you can do about them.

- Reflect on Psalm 71. How do you think this psalm can encourage ageing Christians? Learn to pray the prayer mentioned, be convinced of the hope described, and share the view of service that can be rendered in one's senior years.

Pain and
Suffering

When I was a youth, I came across a story of a king who welcomed his battle-weary sailors home after they had fought valiantly to defend their country. They returned in their badly battered ships and lined up to be received by their king. They stood tall, some missing an eye, others a limb, and many more bearing various injuries and bandages. With tears in his eyes, the king embraced each of them.

If a less than perfect earthly king can welcome his faithful and valiant soldiers in this deeply moving way, how much more will the perfect heavenly King welcome home His faithful saints?

In his old age, Paul had a battered body, carrying the marks of his various trials and sufferings (Galatians 6:17) that had failed to deter him from standing up for Jesus and obeying Him. In his last epistle, he wrote to Timothy, reminding him of his many sufferings for Christ. In particular, he referred to what he endured in Lystra, Timothy's home town.

There Paul had been stoned by a mob and dragged outside the city; everyone thought he was dead. Paul must have lain motionless after suffering this severe, hate-filled stoning instigated by his Jewish enemies. The disciples probably gathered around the still figure of the apostle, praying for him. Amazingly, Paul (most likely bleeding wounds and all) "got up and went back into the city" (Acts 14:20). Such tenacity and endurance in the face of violence must have left a deep impression on the young Timothy, who is reminded by the ageing apostle of the "persecutions I endured" (2 Timothy 3:11).

Instead of complaining that God was "unkind" to him, Paul readily offered thanks when recollecting his many sufferings: "Yet the Lord rescued me from all of them" (2 Timothy 3:11). Paul was eager to talk about God's kindness amidst his hardships. Such was his character. Upon reflecting deeply about all the pain he had to endure, Paul had this to say: "We also glory in our sufferings, because we know that suffering produces perseverance; perseverance, character; and character, hope"

(Romans 5:3–4). Paul was convinced that no pain or suffering comes our way without God's permission, and that in God's economy, no pain is wasted or meaningless. The sufferer is eventually the victor, who gains what cannot be gained otherwise. Christian character helps one endure suffering, and this in turn deepens Christian character.

Paul did not say much about his pain and disabilities arising from the many injuries sustained during the course of faithful ministry. Many scholars believe Paul had eye problems, and perhaps that was the thorn in the flesh he referred to in 2 Corinthians 12:7 (see also Galatians 4:13–15; 6:11). Also, tradition says that he was bow-legged and disfigured because of his injuries. But in the midst of it all, he was thankful to God because his sufferings enabled him to grow in Christlikeness. He was determined to become better, not bitter.

As we age, we also collect many wounds and scars. These are our spiritual medals of honour, if they were received for the sake of Christ. They take the form of social or psychological suffering, giving up a lucrative career, or simply becoming chronically ill because we went to some remote area to spread the fragrance of Christ. As a result, our suffering may grow more pronounced in old age, adding to the normal aches that come with advancing years.

As pain, disability, and suffering increase, it is possible to grow disheartened, and even doubt whether God still cares for us. If and when this happens, it is important to recognise some truths, besides seeking medical help for our conditions:

- We must remember how good God has been to us in the past, and that He will never leave nor forsake us (Deuteronomy 31:6; Hebrews 13:5). Remember His promise that He is working all things together for our good (Romans 8:28).

- Remember that for the Christian, though the going may get more painful by the day, ultimately, there will be a quantum leap into a far better and more glorious day. Paul expressed it in these words: "I consider that our present sufferings are not worth comparing with the glory that will be revealed in us" (Romans 8:18). Such a view of the distant end (no more tears, suffering, and pain; Revelation 21:4) helps us bear with present suffering.

- We need community to help us. It has been

said that a burden shared is a burden halved. Getting together with other ageing saints, who may all be hurting in some way, can be mutually encouraging. We spur one another to persevere and be resilient. Also, those in the larger community (as the one in the local church) can minister to seniors who may need help—praying with them, bringing them to clinics, running errands for them, and just talking to them.

Why do some suffer more than others? We do not know the answers to such questions, but instead of trying to find answers, we must offer our love and understanding. Those who feel that they have been "selected" to suffer more than the rest must stop comparing themselves with others and indulging in self-pity.

The Lord Jesus, when asked by Peter about John after Jesus revealed to Peter how he would suffer, told him simply, "You must follow me" (John 21:22). Each disciple has his own path to walk, carefully chosen by the Lord with all His wisdom and love. Whether we have more pain or less, we must stay on the path and be faithful to the Lord till the end.

Reflect

• Reflect on why pain and suffering are part of life, and especially of Christian discipleship. How has your own experience been in this area, and how do you feel about it?

• Review the three bullet points: God's presence, promise, and people. How do these help when one is facing growing pain and suffering? Think of how you and your church can help seniors in this situation.

Overcoming the
Fear of Death

The year was 1736, and John Wesley was on his way to America to serve as a missionary. Suddenly, his ship was caught in a severe storm and was on the verge of sinking. Wesley realised that, though he was a pastor and missionary, he was afraid to die, like many on the ship.

Wesley then noticed a group of Christians called Moravians. Instead of trembling with uncontrollable fear, they remained calm and sang their beautiful hymns serenely, entrusting their lives to the God they worshipped. Fortunately, the storm died down, and the ship did not sink. All the passengers were safe. But the storm and the fear it struck in Wesley's heart left deeply troubling questions for his soul.

Why do people fear death? It is quite natural. This fear can range from philosophical anxieties about not existing any more to more practical fears about how one would die—perhaps alone in a hospital bed, hooked up to machines and fighting for every breath, or in an aeroplane plunging helplessly towards the sea. Or, the fear could be focused on what would happen after death. Is there such a thing as judgment? Do I have to stand before God? How would I fare? Is there a place called hell for those who do not make it to heaven?

Fears that one is unprepared for death and what lies beyond can also make things worse. Perhaps this fear is expressed in a common dream people have—one is facing an exam or other important task, but is totally unprepared; you have lost your clothes, or your study notes. This kind of dream is probably created by the brain to express the deep fear of being unprepared for death.

How then does one cope with this lingering fear of death? There are numerous suggestions offered by websites and gurus, and most of them involve keeping thoughts of death out of sight and out of mind. But is this a wise thing to do, knowing that death is inevitable, and that it is important to think about it and be prepared for it? To keep it out of our minds is to engage in a form of escapism, which not only *distracts* us from reality, but also *distorts* our perspective of things. Only those who know how to die well will know how to live well. To deny the reality of death is to deny the inevitable truth. Yet many people choose to do so.

What does the Bible say about the fear of death? The Bible brings together two important realities in our lives— *sin* and *death*. When God created the first couple, Adam and Eve, and placed them in the Garden of Eden, He told them that they were free to eat from all the trees, except the tree of the knowledge of good and evil. God had given them free will to trust and obey Him, but tragically they used it to disobey. They sinned when they ate the forbidden fruit. It was not because they were ignorant. The real problem was that they were *disobedient*. They chose to believe Satan's lie that they could live apart from God, that they did not need Him and could be the masters of their own destinies.

God had earlier warned them that if they disobeyed Him, they would *certainly die* (Genesis 2:17). This is reiterated in another part of the Bible, where we read that "the wages of sin is death" (Romans 6:23). This ancient connection that God made between sin and death is deeply embedded in our human memory. We may not understand it intellectually or may even claim not to believe it, but the emotional effects of sensing that connection come to us quite naturally. We carry in our hearts the fear of death because we know that we are sinners, whether we acknowledge it or not. What God warned Adam and Eve about continues to echo in the deep recesses of our souls. People are afraid of dying.

We try to cover up this fear of death by filling our lives with earthly achievements or fleeting entertainment. Sometimes, the nagging fear resurfaces— when we are alone or feeling sad. Then, we plunge ourselves again into mindless activities to drown out the deeply buried fear of death, sweeping it under the carpet of busyness.

But this fear of death stays with us, no matter what distractions we try. The Bible describes people "who all their lives were held in slavery by their fear of death" (Hebrews 2:15). It stays with people all their lives—unless they discover the real solution.

What is the real solution? The real solution to our fear of death is Jesus Christ. There are two main reasons for this: Firstly, *Jesus died for us*. What did Jesus accomplish when He died in our place on the cross? He removed in our lives the curse that was associated with sin and death. By accepting the consequences of our sins on himself, He has removed the sting of death so that we need not feel terrorised or paralysed by it.

Secondly, *Jesus rose from the dead.* The fact that Jesus rose from the dead means that we do not have to fear death. Jesus has broken the curse of sin and transformed death; it is no longer a heavy tombstone sealed shut but a glorious doorway to eternal life. In the words of poet T. S. Eliot, "In my end is my beginning."[95]

Jesus is our Companion. Those who entrust themselves to Him will enjoy His presence. He will become a lifelong and eternal Companion who will walk with us, even through death. "The later years take us into the heart of the central Christian paradox of death/resurrection" and the discovery of God's "winter grace".[96]

Because Jesus has tasted death and returned from it, He is able to accompany us when our turn comes. We observe this precious truth when we read the well-known Psalm 23. The psalmist begins by telling his audience various things about God—how the Lord is his shepherd, who feeds his soul and helps him to walk in righteous paths. Then, when he comes to the "valley of the shadow of death" (v. 4, footnote), the grammar changes. Instead of speaking *about* God, he speaks *to* God: "I will fear no evil, for you are with me; your rod and your staff, they comfort me" (v. 4). The psalmist's audience is gone. Only the Lord Jesus remains with us in the shadow of death.

"We die alone, one at a time."[97] Perhaps that is one reason why people fear death. To travel alone through the unknown can be a frightening prospect. How will you manage what you find on the other side? But when we have Jesus with us, we are not really alone. We have the One who really matters because He is the One who has been through it before, and has come out victorious. He is the perfect guide and companion through death. We need not fear when we have Him by our side.

Reflect

- Why do you think the Bible says that many are held in slavery all their lives by their fear of death (Hebrew 2:15)? What do you think are reasons people fear death and dying? What are your own fears in this regard?

- How can we be freed from the fear of death? What truths and experiences are most helpful? How would you minister to your elderly friends who are afraid of dying?

Bereavement
and Loneliness

The Holmes and Rahe Stress Scale measures the stress an individual is facing. Topping the list of life stresses is the loss of a spouse (100 points). It often comes as a devastating blow, especially when the relationship has been close. It's even worse when the couple have been living in an "empty nest"—there is suddenly an overwhelming sense of loneliness and helplessness.

Old age brings with it potential bereavement; it is something we cannot avoid, unless we are the spouse who dies first. It has been noted that husbands usually die earlier than their wives; there are more widows than widowers. It has also been noted that the surviving spouse may die soon after.

The grieving process that people go through when a loved one dies has been studied extensively. Typically, five stages are described as comprising the grieving process; these are the same in any experience of loss.

- **Stage 1: Denial.** The person uses a psychological defence mechanism to deny that the loved one has died. She is shocked, numbs her feelings, and speaks of the spouse in the present tense, as if he is still around.

- **Stage 2: Anger.** The truth can hit hard when the bereaved person finally faces reality. There may be a sense of frustration and helplessness. Feelings of anger may be directed at doctors ("Why did they not catch it earlier?"), circumstances ("Why did it have to be us?"), God ("Why did you let this happen?), or the departed ("Why did you leave me so soon?").

- **Stage 3: Bargaining.** At this stage, the bereaved person lives in a "What if" and "If only" phase, going through what could have been done or how things could have turned out differently. Feelings of guilt may dominate.

- **Stage 4: Depression.** This is a phase of coming to terms with the painful reality that the loved one has died, and one is now alone. A sense of loneliness and self-pity can make the depression more painful to bear. Symptoms may include trouble sleeping, frequent weeping, loss of appetite and energy, and staying away from others.

- **Stage 5: Acceptance.** The bereaved person comes to accept the new reality, makes necessary adjustments, feels more at peace, and moves forward emotionally and practically in the everyday details of life. Healing takes place.

Sometimes a person may return to earlier stages as part of the healing process, or they may get stuck at a certain stage and find it difficult to move on. It is good to remember that the Lord wept when his friend Lazarus died (John 11:35). He understands what it means to suffer loss and grief, and he "heals the broken-hearted and binds up their wounds" (Psalm 147:3).

One of the major struggles faced in old age is loneliness, which often becomes more acute with the loss of a spouse, close relative, or friend. Loneliness can be a very painful experience that leads to social isolation and depression. It may result in the loss of a healthy self-regard.

Even the apostle Paul felt lonely—when he was immobilised in prison and cut off from his regular social ties. He complained that "no one came to my support, but everyone deserted me" (2 Timothy 4:16; see also 2 Timothy 1:15). Some of his friends had been lured by the distractions of the world or deterred by the danger of associating with him (since he was a political prisoner); others had gone on to do the Lord's work. "Only Luke is with me" wrote Paul (2 Timothy 4:11). He therefore urged Timothy to visit him quickly and to bring along Mark (2 Timothy 4:9, 11).

We may also remember the Old Testament prophet Elijah who, in a moment of exhaustion, loneliness and depression, lamented to God, "I am the only one left" (1 Kings 19:14). But God revealed to him that he had reserved seven thousand brave and faithful people like Elijah, and that he was not alone (1 Kings 19:18).

What can a bereaved or lonely person do to find relief and help? He can consider several suggestions:

- Be honest with yourself about your thoughts and feelings.

- Share with someone close what you are going

through. If you find it difficult to open up to another person, try expressing your feelings by writing them down in a journal.

- Find a group you can be part of. For the bereaved, getting together with others who have also experienced bereavement can be immensely helpful.

- If you are struggling with loneliness, try connecting with others. Some local churches organise day activities for seniors.

- Volunteer your services and get involved with those in need. Reaching out to others with compassion is itself a healing, strengthening, and deeply satisfying experience.

- Give yourself time; healing often takes time.

- Above all, turn to God for company and strength.

Ultimately, God is with us. We may be alone, but we need not ever be lonely, because if we are walking with Christ, He is always with us and will never leave us nor forsake us (Hebrews 13:5).

Reflect

· · · · · · · · · ·

- Psalm 146:9 says that God "sustains the fatherless and the widow". Why does the Bible pay particular attention to the needs of the bereaved (Deuteronomy 14:29; Isaiah 1:17, 23; Acts 6:1; James 1:27)? How can the church minister to those suffering from bereavement?

- Read Romans 8:31–39. How does this passage help one who is struggling with loneliness? What would a ministry to the lonely look like? Is there someone you can reach out with God's love?

Dealing with Depression

A man with sadness written all over his face once entered a stage coach. Inside was a lady who was reading a hymn book and humming a tune. Looking at the man, she asked if he knew the hymn. The man looked at her with great sorrow and said, "Madam, I am the poor unhappy man who wrote that hymn many years ago, and I would give a thousand worlds, if I had them, to enjoy the feelings I had then."[98]

That man was Robert Robertson, who in 1758 wrote the beautiful and inspiring hymn, "Come Thou Fount of Every Blessing". How was it possible for a man who wrote such soul-stirring verse to become so depressed? He is not alone, for there are so many others like him. Christians too can suffer from depression.

William Cowper, one of the great English poets in the 18th century, wrote many wonderful Christian hymns that are still sung today—hymns like "God Moves in Mysterious Ways" and "There is a Fountain Filled with Blood". Yet he suffered frequently from severe depression and had to be cared for by friends. There were times he even questioned whether he was saved.

People like Martin Luther and Charles Spurgeon were also known to have suffered from lifelong depression. Spurgeon, the great preacher of the 19th century, wrote honestly about his regular struggles with depression:

> Knowing by most painful experience what deep depression of spirit means, being visited therewith at seasons by no means few or far between, I thought it might be consolatory to some of my brethren if I gave my thoughts thereon, that younger men might not fancy that some strange thing had happened to them when they became for a season possessed by melancholy; and that sadder men might know that one upon whom the sun has shone right joyously did not always walk in the light.[99]

There are many possible causes of depression. Christian psychologist Archibald Hart describes four types of depression: psychotic, endogenous, neurotic, and reactive.[100]

Psychotic depression is a very serious mental illness, requiring medical treatment, often long-term. Endogenous depression is connected with an imbalance in brain chemistry and is treated with medication that sets right the imbalances. I once counselled a pastor who suffered severe depression and referred him for medical treatment. After a few weeks, he recovered remarkably and told me he had changed his sceptical view of medical treatment for depression. Neurotic depression is connected with personality issues that trigger learned psychological reactions. In stress or anxiety, such a person can become depressed as a way of coping or reacting. Treatment includes counselling and therapy with appropriate medication. Reactive depression is the result of one's personal and social circumstances. Most of us become sad or depressed when things go wrong, when we are disappointed or face failure. When the stressful circumstance is removed, the depression lifts. For example, a person waiting for laboratory tests to confirm if he is suffering from a serious medical condition will become and remain depressed. But when informed that the lab results are normal and there is nothing to worry about, he quickly returns to his old self. Reactive depression is also helped by counselling.

But there is also a kind of depression that can best be termed "spiritual depression".[101] This may be due to the devil's attacks on one's thoughts and moods. It could also be due to spiritual apathy and disobedience. The solution, by definition, has to be spiritual.

Old age brings with it a higher risk of depression. Declining health, bereavement, loneliness, financial concerns, impending death, and regrets may all come together to bring about depression. The senior may feel a loss of energy, appetite, and interest in people and events. Insomnia, negative thoughts and attitudes, and problems remembering and paying attention may make things worse. Also, feelings of helplessness, worthlessness, and hopelessness may break a person down.

Some may feel depressed and socially marginalised with advancing years. Anglican priest Michael Butler and psychotherapist Ann Orbach describe what it's like: "Getting old may feel like acting in a play where the rest of the cast is new and most of the props have changed. There is something familiar about the plot, but we have smaller parts to play, with a lot of time waiting in the wings before making a final bow. For many people, the worst fear is to be 'unwept, unhonoured and unsung', but serenity comes through managing not to mind."[102]

The psalmist asks himself, "Why, my soul, are you downcast? Why so disturbed within me?" (Psalm 42:11). He answers his own question with what he has learned about God—that God is trustworthy and full of love for us. He therefore tells himself, "Put your hope in God, for I will yet praise him, my Saviour and God" (Psalm 42:11).

We may get depressed when we look at ourselves and our circumstances, but when we lift our eyes and thoughts to God, we will see another perspective and receive comfort, courage, and strength. The "twilight time", writes Joan Chittister, "has its own tasks, its burdens, its subtle gifts to give us."[103]

In the same vein, spiritual writer Kathleen Fischer notes that in the case of Abraham and Sarah, we can find the dual themes of humour and human limitation on the one hand, and hope and human possibility on the other.[104] The old couple suffered, not surprisingly, from infertility, and laughed when told that they were about to become parents (Genesis 17:17; 18:12). But God had the last laugh, and when their son was born, they named him "Laughter" (Isaac). God enters our fruitless lives and changes everything.

The two disciples on the road to Emmaus had downcast faces because Jesus had been crucified (Luke

24:17). The risen Christ joined them and explained the Scriptures to them (Luke 24:27). Then He joined them at a meal, and their eyes were opened and they recognised Him (Luke 24:30–31). Their hearts were thrilled and they ran joyfully to the other disciples to tell them the good news. Jesus then appeared to them saying, "Peace be with you," and told them not to be troubled (Luke 24:36–38).

Besides seeking medical help, confiding in others or joining a support group, and taking common sense measures like having good meals and adequate exercise, we must turn ultimately to Christ, who gives us peace.

Reflect

- Reflect on the causes connected with depression and assess whether you have a problem with the condition. If so, what help have you sought and what more can you do?

- How does turning to Christ help us when we are depressed? How would you help someone who is struggling with depression? What would you say and do?

Living with the Fear of Losing Our Memory

A senior leader in a local church, whose ministry was among his fellow seniors, told me about some funny moments in his ministry. He related an incident when a lady in her senior years called him urgently from the airport; she was unable to find her parked car. He drove to the airport and they searched the car park thoroughly, but could not find the car. Finally, he drove her home. When they arrived, they found her car parked there. She had forgotten that she did not drive to the airport. It was a most embarrassing moment for her.

Losing our ability to remember can be humorous at times, but it is also a concern, especially if it becomes more frequent. Tension and frustration mount when considerable effort is needed to remember dates, names, and other details. Coming across people who suffer from dementia and the dreadful and debilitating Alzheimer's disease (which affects memory, language, and thought) may create apprehension in ageing people of the possibility that they too will suffer such serious loss of memory.[105]

What would life be like if you forget most of your key memories? What is a person without his or her memories? Will people lose their identity when they forget who they are or have been?

Whatever our beliefs may be in this matter, the fact remains that the past is connected to the present and future. We live in historical time, and one event leads to another. We cannot ignore yesterday's decisions, relationships, commitments, and experiences.

A disease like Alzheimer's poses several significant theological questions. Will we be able to function properly as human beings if we lose our ability to remember? In a thoughtful book on Alzheimer's disease, Christian historian David Keck directs our attention to the dilemma of people who cannot remember *whose* they are.[106] To forget *whose* you are is to lose your identity.

What a terrifying thought! Keck, writing from personal experience with his mother, an Alzheimer's sufferer, finds a solution in the need for the Christian community to remember our story and past—what Keck calls "churched history".[107] Alzheimer's patients can be sustained through the collective memory of the community.

The biblical tradition places great emphasis on the discipline and act of remembering. The main message of the book of Deuteronomy, in which the word "remember" appears 14 times, is to call Israel to remember God, His covenant with her, and the history of Israel, especially her enslavement to Egypt, the deliverance of the nation and exodus, and her entrance into the Promised Land. Israel got into trouble whenever she forgot her history. Revival came whenever the nation's memory was stirred and she remembered her history and God's dealings with her.

Remembering the past can be both helpful and unhelpful. When people face the great uncertainties of the future, they may cling to the past in a neurotic and obsessive way. When this occurs, a sentimental nostalgia sets in and people get stuck in a glorified past. The past is then absolutized and idolised to such an extent that the future and the present are sacrificed for its sake. In the history of the early church, there were several Jewish Christians who were guilty of clinging to the past in such a way that they were insensitive to the leading of God.

We must avoid the two dangers we have noted—spiritual amnesia and sentimental nostalgia for the past. In other words, we must neither ignore nor idolise the past. Spiritual amnesia, or the loss of memory of God's dealings with us, seems to be the greater danger today, and leads to a loss of our identity. No matter how active and vibrant a church is, without an identity rooted in history, it is doomed to ultimate insignificance. At the same time, the church must avoid a sentimental nostalgia which makes her a prisoner of the past. Amnesia and nostalgia must both be replaced with a proper remembering of God and the story of His people. Such a memory-rich church can offer help to Alzheimer's patients.

In cases of significant memory loss in old age, we can rest in the truth that ultimately, who we are has to do with whose we are. The Christian community can help us remember whose we are through its acts of worship and ministry. Even if those suffering from Alzheimer's disease lose their cognitive abilities to understand these things, the story of the church shared and acted out regularly can help sustain them. From time to time, something in the mists of lost memory may be stirred, when a hymn is sung or a Bible passage is read.

Social memories are fragile and can also fade. But God's memory remains forever. God remembers us (see Genesis 8:1; 19:29; 30:22). We read that the righteous "will be remembered forever" (Psalm 112:6). The one remembering here is God himself. While we may forget who we are, and others may forget us after a while, God's memory of us remains solid. And it is His memory that we can ultimately trust. Because He will remember us forever, we can also have eternal life. Our future is not dependent on our personal and social memories, but on God's divine memory.

Reflect

- What are some fears that seniors have of "losing their minds"? Reflect on your own fears and concerns over this matter. What do you know of advice given by experts to help maintain our cognitive abilities? Read 2 Timothy 4:13. Why do you think Paul requested for his scrolls and parchments (Scriptures, writing and reading material)? What does it say about keeping our intellectual abilities strong in old age?

- Reflect on how the Christian memory and ministry of the church can help individuals who have lost their memory. How are you comforted that God's memory of us will never fade, and how can we entrust ourselves to Him?

Part V:

THINKING OF HEAVEN

What Is Our
Exit Plan?

I was once part of a panel at a special closed door meeting organised for pastors and church leaders in Singapore to discuss the future of the church. Sitting next to me was a respected pastor who was well-known for his leadership in missions and church planting overseas. Just weeks after the meeting, I received the tragic news that he had been killed in a road traffic accident while training pastors in Brazil. He was only in his early sixties and people were shocked. No one could have imagined that this servant of God would end his earthly life in this unexpected way.

How will each of us exit this world? Many will not think very much about it because they are too busy. Wiser ones will know that no one can be sure how they will die, and so there is no point thinking or worrying about it. But many people still hope for a pleasant exit.

In the Bible, there are two men who were taken away from life on earth in a glorious way—without the usual trouble of having to physically die. They are Enoch and Elijah. Enoch was a godly man who "walked faithfully with God" (meaning that he lived a life of constant communion and obedience to God) and at the end of his life he "was no more, because God took him away" (Genesis 5:21–24). The story of Enoch appears in a narrative of men, from Adam to Noah, who had very long life spans ranging from 969 to 365 years (Genesis 5; see Psalm 91:16). The shortest was that of Enoch, which suggests that how long one lives is not as important as how one lives.

Moreover, for all the others, each narrative ends with "and then he died". The only exception was Enoch, suggesting that he did not exit the world the usual way, but was taken by God.

When we read about the prophet Elijah, we get an idea of how this could have taken place. At the end of his life, Elijah was walking with his successor Elisha when "suddenly a chariot of fire and horses of fire appeared and separated the two of them, and Elijah went up to heaven in a whirlwind. Elisha saw this and cried out, 'My father! My father! The chariots and horsemen of Israel!' And

Elisha saw him no more" (2 Kings 2:11–12). That was a glorious and spectacular exit indeed! How we wish we could go like that.

But everyone else in the Bible died in some way, whether due to old age, deadly illness, war, accident, or martyrdom. It is no different in the world we live in. But we still harbour the hope that when our turn comes, it will be a quiet and pain-free exit. We have heard stories of how some people have died at home in their sleep, with no prior serious illness or hospitalisation. And we wish that our own death would be like that.

The truth of the matter is that *how* we die is not in our hands. Scripture declares that our times are in God's hands (Psalm 31:15); and it is into His hands that we can commit our spirits (Psalm 31:5). This was what our Lord Jesus himself prayed to the heavenly Father when He died on the cross (Luke 23:46). His followers, like the first Christian martyr Stephen, prayed the same when they died (Acts 7:59).

God is entirely sovereign in determining how we will end our journey on earth. It may come suddenly, or after a long struggle with illness. It may be painful or peaceful. It is not for us to say how it will be. We can have our preferences, but ultimately we die according to God's will.

The Bible tells us that God not only personally shaped us in our mother's womb ("you knit me together in my mother's womb") but also that "all the days ordained for me were written in your book before one of them came to be" (Psalm 139:13, 16).

God decides how long we will live and how we will die. He does it with all sovereign wisdom, love, and power. We can trust Him to work all things together for our good (Romans 8:28). Though the end may be unpleasant for some, it will not last long. And as we go through the valley of the shadow of death, we will not have to be afraid, for Jesus who once died for us will be there with us. His shepherd's rod and staff will comfort us (Psalm 23:4).

We may not know how we will die, but we know who will be with us when we die. And that's what really matters. That should be our exit plan.

Reflect

· · · · · · · · · ·

- What are some common fears that people have as to how they would die? How do you think there can be relief for such fears, apart from simply denying them?

- Read John 21:18–19. Jesus told Peter how he would die, which would be an unpleasant experience (and tradition holds that Peter was crucified for his faith in Christ). Why do you think Jesus then commanded Peter, "Follow me!"—what would have happened if Peter had not followed Christ? How do you think he would have died? (Hint: To follow Jesus is to have His company even to the end.)

What Will
Heaven Be Like?

Johnny Cash's song "No Earthly Good" contains a line that expresses a popular thought: "But you're so heavenly minded, you're no earthly good." It is possible for Christians to live in a way that does not connect the future heaven with the present earth. But C. S. Lewis helpfully reminds us that this is a false dichotomy. Looking at the most effective Christians in history, he points out: "The Christians who did the most for the present world were just those who thought the most about the next."[108] Thinking about heaven will help us become involved with the world in a redemptive way.

Christians think about heaven in many different ways. One of the questions people ask is: "What will we do in heaven?" Popular culture often depicts people in heaven as lazing around on clouds, leisurely playing their harps. This idea probably has biblical roots, for the book of Revelation does speak about clouds and harps (Revelation 5:8, 14:2, 14; 15:2). There is also the notion that we will all be one eternal choir praising God—just look at all the heavenly songs in Revelation. This usually begins as a great thought, especially for those who love singing, but after a while, even they ask, "But what else will we do in heaven?"

The problem is that we may be approaching the subject from the wrong angle. Even thoughts that begin with biblical passages can be hijacked by mindsets that are dominated by worldly culture. Yes, the Bible does speak about harps and clouds, and about heavenly singing. But if we see them as nothing more than actions or activities, then we have misunderstood what the Bible actually teaches.

Our problem is that we have become captive to a pragmatic way of thinking that has been absorbed into our way of life in every sphere. We have uncritically embraced utilitarianism.[109] We therefore tend to measure ourselves by what we do or achieve, and judge others in the same way. This is reflected in every conceivable area of life. Take, for instance, going on holiday. We tend to be obsessed with what our holiday destination has to offer in terms of attractions. We are terrified by the thought of becoming bored with nothing to do. The problem is that we in the modern age tend to define ourselves by our "doing".

Those who see the inadequacy of such a perspective try to find a more satisfying basis—by exploring what was the dominant way of thinking in the pre-modern era. Then, the focus was more on being rather than doing. We were defined by who we were rather than what we did. Thus, we have people who remind us today that we ought to focus on *being* rather than *doing*, that our Christian lives really have to do with who we become, rather than what we achieve. This is immediately helpful and a much-needed corrective in a culture infected by an activism that makes us run in meaningless circles. Let us stop and think about what sort of people we are, and are becoming.

Perhaps we can approach the question of heaven from this angle: asking what we will do is not as important as thinking about what we will be in heaven. However, even here, we will face limitations, for we know ourselves. The human condition, as pointed out by Thomas Oden, includes boredom (as well as anxiety and guilt).[110] If we are left to ourselves, we will soon hit rock bottom and become bored. Just lock yourself in a room for a few weeks with nothing else to do and no one to talk to, and you will understand this.

This brings us to what the Bible really teaches. The biblical worldview is that we are defined not by what we do or achieve, and not even by who we are, but by whose we are. We are defined by who we are with. The core of existence is not doing or even being, but *being with*. That is why Jesus warns disciples that judgement will have to do with *being with* rather than *doing* per se (Matthew 7:21–23).

When Paul, the ageing apostle, was imprisoned in Rome, he no doubt thought much about what would happen to him. Would he be martyred, or would God allow him to continue his ministry for a few more years? In his letter to the Philippians, he reveals some of these thoughts: "I am torn between the two: I desire to depart and *be with Christ*, which is better by far; but it is more necessary for you that I remain in the body . . . so that through my *being with you* again your boasting in Christ Jesus will abound on account of me" (Philippians 1:23–26, emphasis added).

For Paul, heaven was defined as *being with Christ*. The alternative was *being with God's people*. In putting it this way, Paul summarised the heart of Christian living— which is being with the Lord and His people. Another way this is seen is in what the Lord himself taught—

that the heart of the Law is love for God and neighbour (Matthew 22:37–40). The call to Christian discipleship is a call to enter into holy and loving relationships with God and others. It is essentially a relational matter.

We now return to our previous questions about heaven. What will heaven be like? Paul quoted Isaiah by declaring: "What no eye has seen, what no ear has heard, and what no mind has conceived—the things God has prepared for those who love him" (1 Corinthians 2:9). No one can fully imagine or even accurately depict how heaven will be like for us. But Paul did add a clause immediately after his quote from Isaiah: "these are the things God has revealed to us by his Spirit" (1 Corinthians 2:10).

We now have some idea of how heaven will be like. It should not be conceived of in terms of what we will do, or even who we will be, but rather who we will *be with* (Revelation 21:3). We must approach heaven not with a "to do" list or in terms of some Gnostic idea of self-fulfilment, but rather in terms of relationship. In heaven, we will be with the eternal God who created and saved us, who sustains us moment by moment. He is an infinitely creative Being in whose presence we will not get bored. We will get bored with activities and ourselves but we will never get bored with the eternal God. His love will remove our deep boredom.

This much we know from Scripture. We already have a brief description of heaven. The reality, however, awaits us in the future, and we can look forward to it with great anticipation. And yes, we will sing, but in a state of self-forgetfulness and without needing to check our watches, in the presence of divine majesty.

Reflect

- What are your favourite thoughts about heaven? What are some questions you have? Discuss these with other Christians, and explore how our thoughts of heaven can be shaped by what Scripture teaches.

- As we age, we realise that it would not be long before we are in our eternal home. How would you think about heaven, and how would such thoughts bring you peace and hope?

Preparing for Heaven

I knew a church member who could tell you the exact number of holes on the church communion rail for placing used cups. He had taken the trouble to count the perforations, and I wonder how many times he had to count them to make sure he got it right. Unfortunately, this man passed away before we could find out other interesting facts about the church building and its furnishings. The man was good at counting, but did he count the most important things?

Psalm 90, attributed to Moses, is probably the oldest psalm in the Bible. In it, we read a petition: "Teach us to number our days *aright*, that we may gain a heart of wisdom" (Psalm 90:12 NIV1984, emphasis added). It is critical that we count our days aright, which means to count them correctly, no matter what else we are drawn to count. But how do we do it? It is not easy; otherwise the psalmist would not have had to ask God to teach him to count. Apparently, it's more challenging than calculating one's trophies, calorie intake, discount savings, or bank accounts.

The difficulty in counting our days can be understood when we realise that the psalmist is referring to the finitude of our lives on earth—"Our days may come to seventy years, or eighty, if our strength endures" (Psalm 90:10). We all have an expiry date—the trouble is, we do not know when that is. We know our birth date, but not the day when we shall breathe our last. And, if the psalmist is really talking about *counting down* rather than counting, we can appreciate the particular difficulty at hand. It is easy to count our age and the years we have lived, but it is difficult to count our remaining days since we don't know when the end will come.

To count our days aright is to realise that our remaining days are numbered—and it is not really a big number. To count our days correctly does not mean arriving at a particular number, it means arriving at true wisdom, a wisdom that knows the implications of limited time on earth. Such wisdom will enable us to see our days on earth and all they entail in the context of eternity with God in

His kingdom. As we read in the well-known Psalm 23, we often think about the phrase "all the days of my life" (Psalm 23:6) and long for all our days on earth to be richly blessed with God's goodness and love. But this would be true only if all our days are framed in the "forever" reality of the "house of the LORD" (Psalm 23:6).

Only as we turn to the eternal God saying: "from everlasting to everlasting you are God" (Psalm 90:2), can we really learn to count our days aright. *Our limited days must be properly framed within the eternal years of God*; then only can we find true meaning for our passing and transient days. Godly wisdom will know how to differentiate the ultimate from the penultimate, the number of perforations in the communion rail from the life-transforming encounter with the living Christ.

Many people encounter a problem here. They spend a good part, if not all, of their days worrying and running after functional penultimate goals. They have difficulty knowing the difference between means and ends, between that which will crumble into dust and that which will endure. Jesus told His listeners: "do not worry about your life, what you will eat or drink; or about your body, what you will wear . . . your heavenly Father knows that you need them. But seek first his kingdom and his righteousness, and all these things will be given to you as well" (Matthew 6:25, 32–33).

Jesus also told the story of an unnamed rich man and a beggar named Lazarus (Luke 16:19–31). The story itself is radical. Both rich men and beggars must die, but their lot on the other side can be vastly different from that on earth. The rich man had the skills to count his wealth and possessions. Even on the other side, he could still count (he mentions his five brothers), and he expects Lazarus to be like a servant to him when he asks Abraham to send him over with some water! The man had not changed, for his sinful character had become frozen and hardened on the other side.

Lazarus must also have counted his days. His days on earth were extremely miserable; he lived in the shadows of the margins, and his sores refused to heal. He must have told himself that the end was surely not far away, that his sufferings would soon be over. The rich man, on the other hand, thought that there would be no end to his pleasures. He did not have the godly wisdom to count his days.

When we count our days aright, we will be blessed in many ways. First, we will experience deep satisfaction from knowing God personally, for He satisfies us every morning with His unfailing love (Psalm 90:14). There is no greater satisfaction in life than knowing with certainty that God loves us perfectly. He knows what we need and will give it to us. He will not leave us stranded or forgotten.

Second, even amid affliction, we can experience gladness (Psalm 90:15). We are able to say with Paul, "I consider that our present sufferings are not worth comparing with the glory that will be revealed in us" (Romans 8:18). Godly wisdom knows that there is value in suffering, for "suffering produces perseverance; perseverance, character; and character, hope" (Romans 5:3–4). We are not victims of circumstances but "patients" of God, who is remaking us into something that is likely to be beyond our imagination!

Third, God's presence in our lives will continue in the following generations (Psalm 90:16). We will be enabled to live wisely so that God's splendour will be shown to our children too. We will have the joy of knowing that God has been at work not only in our lives but also in those who come after us. God is not only the God of Abraham, but also of Isaac and Jacob.

Fourth, the work that we do for the Lord will endure (Psalm 90:17). Wisely done labour for the Lord will not be in vain (1 Corinthians 15:58). We can have the confidence that it is really God who is at work, putting everything together for our good and His glory (Romans 8:28). Work carried out with godly wisdom will survive into eternity (1 Corinthians 3:14).

In short, the wisdom that we read about in Psalm 90 leads to peace in the heart, even amid setbacks, as we come to know God deeply. Our blessings will endure in the lives of others as we leave behind a legacy in the service we do for the Lord. All this wisdom comes from knowing how to count our days aright.

The ancient St Catherine's monastery at the foot of Mount Sinai marks the spot where Moses (who wrote Psalm 90) met God at the burning bush. Monks have been living there for the last 1,500 years. When they die, they are buried for a while, and then their bones are unearthed and kept in the chapel. Visitors will find heaps of skulls gathered over the centuries. They serve to remind the monks that their days on earth need to be framed by eternity. The skull heaps quietly articulate that ancient prayer: Teach us to count our days.

Our churches today have no skull heaps nor graveyards (which are common in old churches across Europe) to give us wisdom, and although some have columbaria, these tend to be disconnected from the regular life of the churches. Still, as congregations, we must collectively and individually seek to live wisely, learning to count down our days, and looking forward to the days that cannot be counted in the "forever" reality of God. As the years pass us by, let us learn to frame our days with the eternity of God.

Reflect

- How does learning to count our days aright help us prepare for heaven? What would this entail for you personally? How can you learn to count your days aright?

- Knowing how to count our days aright helps us to live our remaining days wisely. What characterises such a wisely-lived life? How should our days on earth be made meaningful and framed by God's eternity? Examine your own life in this light.

Harbouring Hope

A pastor in East Malaysia told me about an American missionary couple who had served the Lord in that region for many years, planting churches, discipling many, and blessing countless people. They had retired to America and were in their 80s when some of the Christian leaders in Sabah arranged for them to visit the land of their missionary service. They came with much joy and were greeted by grateful crowds, who fondly thanked them for blessing them greatly. In one place, they lined a street to welcome the missionaries. After the celebrations, the missionary gentleman told the pastor, "You know, after this, there is nothing else to look forward to on earth." Shortly after their return to the US, the man died and went home to the Lord.

The pastor related how for the last 5 years of his life, the missionary spoke increasingly about heaven. Near the end of his life, it was as if there was nothing else he could talk about. This servant of God had a living hope. He knew that his time to leave earth and arrive at his eternal home in Christ was near, and he was excited about it. It was as if he had already "packed his bags" and sent them off to heaven. He was just waiting for the transport.

Old age brings with it all kinds of challenges, as we have already seen. There are illnesses to struggle with, the sense of the end, perhaps loneliness and depression, and fears regarding the future. But for the Christian, who believes in Christ and walks with Him, there is always hope. Christ will have the final say in our lives. And He will say, as God said after creating all things, "It is good". He works all things together for our good (Romans 8:28), and will give the final verdict, pronouncing what He has created out of the ups and downs of our lives as "Good!"

If He is for us, who can be against us, and what can separate us from His love (Romans 8:31, 35)? Our God is described as the "God of hope" who fills us with joy and peace that we are not able to find elsewhere. Paul prayed for the Christians in Rome, "May the God of hope fill you with all joy and peace as you trust in him, so that you may overflow with hope by the power of the Holy Spirit" (Romans 15:13). He is the one who gives us endurance and encouragement (Romans 15:5), even as we face the challenges of this life. He can be trusted, and as we do so, He will give us His peace, joy, and hope.

J. I. Packer describes the condition of many old people in Western society, who have no faith and hope:

> One of the saddest things today is the number of elderly people who, not being believers, have nothing to look forward to. Their life is fading away. Their bodies are getting feeble and breaking down. They cannot do what they used to, and will never be able to do it again. They feel they are moving deeper into a dark cave with the darkness thickening around them, and no light, or way out, for them at the end. They find living without hope to be an unrelieved burden. They get bitter in heart, and sunk in self-pity and nostalgia. If they become (as, alas, they sometimes do) a misery to others, it is because they first became in this way a misery to themselves. Hopelessness wastes the spirit.[111]

It is a dreadful situation to turn old and helpless without any hope for the future. But for the child of God, there is always hope, because we are moving towards a glorious future. We do not have it yet, nor have we already arrived. It is awaiting us, like light at the end of the tunnel.

Robert Browning's poem encourages the old and reminds them of their hope in God.

> *Grow old along with me*
> *The best is yet to be.*
> *The last of life, for which the first was made;*
> *Our times are in his hand*
> *Who saith, "A whole I planned,*
> *Youth shows but half: trust God: see all, be not afraid.*[112]

Paul describes how we wait for our full redemption in Christ, and writes, "For in this hope we were saved. But hope that is seen is no hope at all. Who hopes for what they already have? But if we hope for what we do not yet have, we wait for it patiently" (Romans 8:24–25).

It is with this same spirit that Paul also testified, "Forgetting what is behind and straining towards what is ahead, I press on towards the goal to win the prize for which God has called me heavenwards in Christ Jesus" (Philippians 3:13–14). Adam Clarke used stirring words to describe how Paul anticipates impending death: "he now appears, standing on the verge of eternity, full of God, and strongly anticipating an eternity of glory."[113] To die full of God and hope is to die well.

For the Christian, the future neither holds nothing, nor more of the same; rather, it holds the best, for in the future, there will be no more pain, death, failure, or disappointment, and everything will be renewed by Christ (Revelation 21:4–5).

Thus, we have to learn, with the power of the Holy Spirit, to endure and be encouraged as we wait in eager expectation.

Joni Eareckson Tada, who was paralysed at a young age due to an accident, lives in this way that glorifies God and ministers to many. She wrote about the kind of hope that she had personally experienced through pain, suffering, and disability. "The best we can hope for in this life is a knothole peek at the shining realities ahead. Yet a glimpse is enough. It's enough to convince our hearts that whatever sufferings and sorrows currently assail us aren't worthy of comparison to that which waits over the horizon."[114]

A Christian who has walked with Christ faithfully till old age would have received more than a fair share of such knothole peeks at the future that awaits us, for God has revealed to us in part what He has prepared for us, beyond our imagination (1 Corinthians 2:9–10). We know that Christ "will transform our lowly bodies so that they will be like his glorious body" (Philippians 3:21).

Let us therefore remember the resurrection of Christ and be filled with this "living hope", knowing that in Christ, an inheritance is kept in heaven for us (1 Peter 1:3–4). We would do well to heed the wise advice of Oswald Chambers:

> Remember Whose you are and Whom you serve. Provoke yourself by recollection, and your affection for God will increase tenfold; your imagination will not be starved any longer, but will be quick and enthusiastic, and your hope will be inexpressibly bright.[115]

Reflect

- Why is God called the "God of hope" (Romans 15:13)? How can a senior find hope in Christ amid worsening circumstances? How would you help someone who has lost hope?

- What does it mean to have a "living hope" (1 Peter 1:3) and what sort of inheritance do you think awaits us in heaven? In what way would it be totally different from our earthly experiences? How does this encourage you? Find opportunities to share this with elderly friends and those who are suffering.

Being a
Blessing

Most people want to be blessed in life. Fewer people seek to be a blessing in life.

This is not surprising as the self is the most important reality for most people. Everyone is born with a full sense of self. Scientists tell us that a newborn baby is only aware of himself, and that everybody, including the mother, is perceived as an extension of that self. There is no sense of distinction between self and the other. The infant soon recognises others apart from himself. But most children still grow up with the self as the most important reality. They will then tend to use others for their own self-centred purposes and agendas. They also tend to use God in the same way.

Most people begin their journey of faith in the same way. They realise there is a God above themselves, then try to use Him for their own well-being. The medieval monk Bernard of Clairvaux called this "loving God for our own sake".[116] It takes some time in the faith journey before we discover a deeper layer where we learn to "love God for His sake". Between the two stages is a Copernican revolution of sorts, where self is no longer at the centre of our universe. Instead, God takes His rightful place as the central reality of our existence.

When this takes place, we become less self-centred and self-absorbed, and begin to relate to God and others in a self-giving way. When we turn to God in this way, we discover true worship. When we turn to those around us in a self-giving way, we discover true service; we become a blessing to others.

As we age, we should be discovering these important stages in our spiritual journey. A certain sense of contentment should mark our path. It is great gain (1 Timothy 6:6; Hebrews 13:5) and something we can learn to experience whatever our circumstances (Philippians 4:11–12). This experience of contentment and gratitude becomes the springboard of true service.

When God called Abraham, He told the man, "I will bless those who bless you . . . and all peoples on earth will be blessed through you" (Genesis 12:3). We must note the connection here. God blesses us, and as a result, we become a blessing to others. We are not to become selfish reservoirs, but generous channels through which God's blessings flow into the lives of others.

A geographical lesson from Israel is sometimes used to illustrate this. There are two big lakes in Israel: the Dead Sea and the Sea of Galilee. The Dead Sea is far below sea level and collects all the water flowing in from the Jordan River. Because the water does not flow out, the lake has become stagnant and lifeless—hence its name.

On the other hand, the Sea of Galilee is teeming with life and has vegetation, towns, and cities on its shores. As it was in Jesus' day, it is a place where fish are caught commercially. The Sea of Galilee has water flowing both into and out. When God called Abraham, He intended the patriarch to be like the Sea of Galilee—being blessed and being a blessing.

As we age, we have probably collected more blessings than younger people. One popular local saying is: "I have eaten more salt than you have eaten rice," meaning, "I have more experience of life than you". This is often said by an older person to the young. Yes, there are joys and sorrows in life, but blessings come in many forms, and if we paused to count our blessings, we would realise we have an overwhelming number of them. This should create a living stream of gratitude in us, and, as Adrian van Kaam and Susan Muto point out, "ageing gracefully is impossible without gratefulness".[117] We may remember Johnson Oatman Junior's hymn,

> *When upon life's billows you are tempest-tossed,*
> *When you are discouraged, thinking all is lost,*
> *Count your many blessings, name them one by one,*
> *And it will surprise you what the Lord has done.*

If we have been blessed as such, we should also be thinking of others, and more so as we age. Why not prayerfully thank God for His blessings and start making a list of people in whose lives we can be a blessing? It could be a family member, churchgoer, other seniors, and those we meet in the market, hospital, train, and so many other places.

How can one be a blessing to others? We may have slowed down in old age but there are still so many ways we can be a blessing to others.

We can be available to others to lend a listening ear, offer a healing or encouraging word, or perform a kind act. We can conduct Bible study with a group, like our family, or with individuals. We can pass good books on for others to read. We can smile when others around us are frowning, or talk to those who are lonely or neglected. We can use our resources for mission work. We can simply pray for others.

An old proverb states, "There is only one crime worse than murder in the desert, and that is to know where the water is and not tell." We can be a great blessing to others when we make use of opportunities to tell them about the Jesus who saves us and satisfies our soul-quenching thirst. A senior could pray like this (from H. Glen Lanier's hymn "For All the Joys of Living"):

> Let not the fear of ageing
> Consume our future days;
> Give us the daily courage, Lord,
> To serve in untried ways.
>
> Keep us from weak complaining,
> Of years that now are gone;
> May insights gained each passing year
> Be light to lead us on.[118]

Is it possible that in heaven, as each person is called to stand before God, others who have been a blessing to them will also be called to stand alongside? Who would stand with you? These would be people who have blessed you; some well-known, others you didn't even realise were used by God to bless you.

When others are called, will you be called as one who has been a blessing to them? Imagine the joy if this happens, especially if you are called upon many times!

Reflect

- What has maturity got to do with moving away from self-centredness to focusing on others—God and those around us? How will this be experienced both in terms of worship (God-centeredness) and service (seeking to bless others)?

- How can a senior learn to focus on being a blessing to others? What everyday opportunities to do this come your way? Learn to look through the eyes of Jesus and identify those to whom you can be a channel of blessing. Who are these people?

Leaving
a Legacy

How will we be remembered after we leave?
Eulogies at funerals usually contain nice words
about the deceased, much of which are easily forgotten
with the passage of time. After all, how many of us
remember ancestors beyond our own grandparents or
great-grandparents? Social memory does fade over time.
Tombstones become neglected. So, why think about
leaving a legacy behind?

The strange thing is that if we focus on leaving behind
a legacy, our efforts will be no more than acts of self-
praise that dissipate with time. But if we focus on loving
and obeying Christ, then we will leave behind something
significant and lasting. To reflect more on this, let us look
at the example of Christ himself.

We may begin by asking the question, "What did Jesus leave behind?" Jesus did not leave behind a family (wife and children), house, property, bank account, business, monument, portrait, book, physical remnant, or gravestone. Dr James Allen Francis' poem, *One Solitary Life*, describes how Jesus did not have the kind of things that people usually associate with a legacy.

> He was born in an obscure village, the child of a peasant woman. He grew up in another village, where He worked in a carpenter shop until He was thirty. Then for three years He was an itinerant preacher. He never wrote a book. He never held an office. He never had a family or a home. He didn't go to college. He never visited a big city. He never travelled two hundred miles from the place where He was born. He did none of the things that usually accompany greatness. He had no credentials but Himself.
>
> He was only thirty-three when the tide of public opinion turned against Him. His friends ran away. One of them denied Him. He was turned over to His enemies and went through the mockery of a trial. He was nailed to a cross between two thieves.

While He was dying, His executioners gambled for His garments, the only property He had on earth. When He was dead, He was laid in a borrowed grave through the pity of a friend.

Nineteen centuries have come and gone, and today He is the central figure of the human race. All the armies that ever marched, all the navies that ever sailed, all the parliaments that ever sat, all the kings that ever reigned, put together, have not effected the life of man on this earth as much as that One Solitary Life.[119]

So what did Jesus leave behind? In short, His *teachings* and His *church*. Jesus declared, "Heaven and earth will pass away, but my words will never pass away" (Matthew 24:35). He also said, "I will build my church, and the gates of Hades will not overcome it" (Matthew 16:18).

The Lord encountered crowds, which were a common feature of His relatively short ministry on earth. Among these, He left behind many who were touched by His ministry—the blind, lame, dumb, and even those who had died and were raised by Him. More importantly, Jesus left behind disciples. There were 120 believers in the Upper Room (Acts 1:15) who waited for Pentecost. Of these, Jesus particularly trained the Twelve, and spent considerable time with them. The apostles spread the gospel around the world, wrote or were instrumental in the writing of the Scriptures, and died as martyrs. They were not the best of men, but Jesus did His miracle of transforming them, correcting their blindness and slowness of spirit. Jesus gave His disciples three realities.

First, He gave them His *Holy Spirit*. The Spirit is connected to Jesus. He promised them the filling of the Spirit (which was achieved at Pentecost, and this filling transformed the apostles). The Spirit would produce holiness in them (the character of Christ) and enable them to carry on the ministry of Jesus. The Spirit of Jesus is His lasting legacy because the Holy Spirit will be with us forever (John 14:16).

While we are not Jesus, and we do not impart the Holy Spirit like Jesus did, nevertheless, the lesson for us is that we can leave behind the spirit that characterised our lives—the legacy we leave behind represents our character, attitudes, ministry, and so on—it is a living legacy.

Second, Jesus gave His disciples His *teachings*. Jesus taught with authority, like no other (Mark 1:22). He left behind a certain worldview, a certain way of looking at the Old Testament, and a certain way of faith and life. All this is concretely captured in the New Testament. Jesus left behind His Word. The implication for us is that we too can leave behind what shaped our lives—our beliefs, values, principles, and precepts for living.

Third, Jesus left behind His *peace* to His disciples. The risen Jesus greeted His disciples with "Peace be with you" (Luke 24:36; John 20:19, 26). Jesus did not promise a stress-free life; there will be troubles. In John 16:33, He says that "in this world you will have trouble" but also that "in me you may have peace". This is the legacy that Jesus has left behind that has inspired so many and has been demonstrated in the lives of so many down the centuries.

Jesus left behind a people and His Word that He gave to them. He also gave them His Spirit and His peace. If these are the emphases of Jesus, should they not be reflected in our own legacies—in how we invest our lives and spend our days and energies?

Eugene Bianchi suggests, "Perhaps the most beautiful legacy that ageing parents can leave their children is a personally lived lesson about facing old age and death with courage and grace."[120] We can think of both biological and spiritual children here.

Adam Clarke wrote of believers in Christ, you "are immortal till your work is done."[121] This statement was deeply encouraging to me when I was diagnosed with pancreatic cancer in 2012. My doctors were ready to perform surgery, but I sought a second opinion overseas on the biopsy results. Three weeks later, the second opinion came back, saying it was not likely to be cancer. The surgery was thankfully cancelled.

The experience led me to reflect on why God keeps us alive. I realised that our work is really the result of God's work. Every new day, we should ask ourselves, why has God kept me alive today? I have learned two answers to that question. First, God's work *in* me is not over—this has to do with my becoming Christlike. Second, God's work *through* me is not over—this has to do with my ministry for Christ. On the day God takes me home, I will know that His work in me and through me is finished—to His glory.

What a splendid truth! Because God is working in us and through us, as we cooperate with God and let Him reproduce Christ's character and ministry in our lives, we will leave behind a living legacy shaped by His grace and power.

Reflect

· · · · · · · · · ·

- Reflect on the legacy that Jesus left behind. What personal lessons are there for you? What do your reflections tell you about how you should live and what you should focus on?

- Think of some people you knew who have departed from this life, and who have left behind a good legacy. What features of their legacy do you appreciate? What do they say about their beliefs, values, relationships, and priorities in life? How do these legacies bring glory to God?

Epilogue

"What good is it to live a long life when we amend that life so little?" Thomas à Kempis asks this thought-provoking question in his classic *The Imitation of Christ*.[122] The question is important and it will either make someone try harder or give up completely.

Imagine you are stuck in traffic, inching forward at a crawling pace that tests your patience. What if you give up and pull up by the side of the road? Life can be like that. You find that you are not making much progress. In spite of listening to countless sermons and inspiring talks, you find that your life has become stagnant. Old age can bring with it increasing scepticism, and you may just give up the whole "spiritual journey thing", and just seek to enjoy life as it comes. (A note to preachers: how important it is to learn how to preach edifying and meaningful sermons to seniors in the church).[123]

But if you persist and remain in the journey, you will make progress, no matter how slow or small. After a jam, the traffic inevitably starts flowing again, and you will eventually reach your destination. The key is to stay in the journey, and in the Christian life, this is done through obedience, the putting into practice of whatever we hear from God.

At the end of His Sermon on the Mount (Matthew 5–7), Jesus told the parable of the two men who build their houses. The wise man builds his house on solid rock, while the foolish man takes the easy way out and builds his house on the sand. Eventually it rains heavily, and the flood waters rise. The house on the rock remains standing while the other one collapses.

The difference between the two builders is explained by Jesus. "Therefore everyone who hears these words of mine and puts them into practice is like a wise man who built his house on the rock . . . But everyone who hears these words of mine and does not put them into practice is like a foolish man who built his house on sand" (Matthew 7:24, 26). *The difference is whether we put into practice what we hear.*

The apostle Paul says the same thing, with an appeal to urgent and consistent action. "Keep putting into practice all you learned and received from me—everything you heard from me and saw me doing. Then the God of peace will be with you" (Philippians 4:9 NLT).

As age catches up with us, we do not have the luxury of time. We must avoid the situation where we are "always learning but never able to come to a knowledge of the truth" (2 Timothy 3:7). We can only grow in our knowledge of truth through faith and obedience that are consistently exercised. J. I. Packer, the wise and aged theologian, advises that in the last lap of our lives, we must "live for God one day at a time", remembering the line from a hymn written in 1674 by Bishop Thomas Ken— "Live each day as if thy last".[124]

We also have God's promise, on which we can rest:

> *Even to your old age and grey hairs*
> *I am he, I am he who will sustain you.*
> *I have made you and I will carry you;*
> *I will sustain you and I will rescue you. (Isaiah 46:4)*

Let us therefore gain insight and our true inheritance in Christ. In the words of Dag Hammarskjöld, we can say with gratitude to God and hope in Christ, "Night is drawing nigh; for all that has been, thanks; for all that shall be, yes."[125]

Endnotes

1   Frits de Lange, *Loving Later Life: An Ethics of Aging* (Grand Rapids: William B. Eerdmans, 2015), 4. See also Heather E. Dillaway and Mary Byrnes, "Reconsidering Successful Aging: A Call for Renewed and Expanded Academic Critiques and Conceptualizations", *Journal of Applied Gerontology* 28, no. 6 (December 2009), 702–722.

2   Carole Bailey Stoneking, "Modernity: The Social Construction of Aging", in *Growing Old in Christ*, eds. Stanley Hauerwas, Carole Bailey Stoneking, Keith G. Meador, and David Cloutier (Grand Rapids: William B. Eerdmans, 2003), 63.

3   See Robert Raines, *A Time to Live: Seven Tasks of Creative Aging* (New York: Dutton, 1997), where he lists the seven tasks: waking up (to our mortality and spiritual needs), embracing sorrow (acknowledging losses and pain and growing in compassion), savouring blessedness (remembering how we have been blessed and can be a blessing), re-imagining work (fulfilling vocation), nurturing intimacy (with family and friends), seeking forgiveness (entering old age with minimum baggage), and taking on the mystery (accepting life and death and exploring the ultimate meaning of life with thanksgiving and hope). See also Kenneth Stokes, "A Growing Faith After 60", *Alert* 12, no. 4 (1983), 11–13, where he mentions four faith tasks of older adulthood: adjusting to retirement and loss of power, keeping mentally and spiritually alert, adjusting to changing cultural values and patterns, and personal preparation for death.

4   R. Paul Stevens, *Aging Matters: Finding Your Calling for the Rest of Your Life* (Grand Rapids: William B Eerdmans, 2006), 67; Dallas Willard, *The Spirit of the Disciplines: Understanding How God Changes Lives* (San Francisco: Harper and Row, 1988), 156.

5   Ibid., 15.

6   Gordon MacDonald, *Who Stole My Church? What to Do When the Church You Love Tries to Enter the 21st Century* (Nashville: Thomas Nelson, 2007).

7   Henri J. M. Nouwen and Walter J. Gaffney, *Aging: The Fulfillment of Life* (Garden City, NY: Image Books, 1976), 154.

8   George MacDonald, "The Marquis of Lossie", in *Delphi Complete Works of George MacDonald*, (Hastings, England: Delphi, 2015), 5832.

9   Brian Christopher Coulter, *Be Holy: Find Identity, Find Belonging, Find Purpose* (St. Louis, MO: Chalice Press, 2014), 40–41.

10   Eugene Bianchi, *Aging as a Spiritual Journey* (New York: Crossroads, 1992), 190.

11   There are many modern language editions of *The Pilgrim's Progress*, which was first published by John Bunyan in 1678. See John Bunyan, *Pilgrim's Progress* (Abbotsford, WI: Life Sentence, 2014).

12   G. K. Chesterton, *What's Wrong with the World?* (New York: Sheed and Ward, 1956), http://www.gkc.org.uk/gkc/books/whats_wrong.html.

13 *The Shepherd of Hermas*, Ante-Nicene Fathers, vol. 2 (Grand Rapids: William B. Eerdmans, 1962).

14 Leo E. Missinne, *Reflections on Aging: A Spiritual Guide* (Liguori, MO: Ligouri, 1990), 106.

15 Bruce Barton, *What Can a Man Believe?* (Indianapolis: Bobbs-Merrill, 1927), 252–253.

16 Søren Kierkegaard, *Purity of Heart Is to Will One Thing* (New York: Harper and Brothers, 1938).

17 T. S. Eliot, *Knowledge and Experience in the Philosophy of F. H. Bradley* (New York: Columbia University Press, 1964), 23.

18 Stevens, *Aging Matters*, chap. 5.

19 James M. Houston and Michael Parker, *A Vision for the Aging Church: Renewing Ministry for and by the Seniors* (Downers Grove, IL: IVP Academic, 2011), 23.

20 Jane Marie Thibault and Richard L. Morgan, *Pilgrimage into the Last Third of Life: 7 Gateways to Spiritual Growth* (Nashville: Upper Room Books, 2012), 15.

21 Homer L. Jernigan and Margaret B. Jernigan, *Aging in Chinese Society: A Holistic Approach to the Experience of Aging in Taiwan and Singapore* (New York: Haworth Press, 1992), chap. 5.

22 Ibid, 102.

23 Oliver James, *Affluenza* (London: Vermillion, 2007), vii.

24 Warren W. Wiersbe, *Living with the Giants* (Grand Rapids: Baker, 1993), 172.

25 John Stott, *The Radical Disciple* (Nottingham: Inter-Varsity Press, 2010), 32.

26 Eugene H. Petersen, *The Jesus Way: A Conversation in Following Jesus* (London: Hodder and Stoughton, 2007), 7.

27 Dallas Willard, *Renovation of the Heart: Putting on the Character of Christ* (Colorado Springs: NavPress, 2002), 159.

28 Dag Hammarskjöld, *Markings*, trans. Leif Sjoberg and W. H. Auden (New York: Alfred A. Knopf, 1964), 56.

29 David J. Maitland, *Aging as Counterculture: A Vocation for the Later Years* (New York: Pilgrim Press, 1991), 14.

30 Ibid., 137, 145.

31 Abba Moses, "Moses 2", in *Sayings of the Desert Fathers: The Alphabetical Collection*, trans. Benedicta Ward (London: A. R. Mowbray, 1975), 138–139.

32 John Duckworth, *Joan n the Whale: And Other Stories You Never Heard in Sunday School* (Eastbourne, England: Monarch, 1987), 100–103.

33 J. Dwight Pentecost, *Life's Problems—God's Solutions: Answers to Fifteen of Life's Most Perplexing Problems* (Grand Rapids: Kregel, 1971), 76.

34 Bell Hooks, *All About Love: New Visions* (New York: Harper Perennial, 2001), 4; Gary Chapman, *Love Is a Verb: Stories of What Happens When Love Comes Alive* (Minneapolis, MN: Bethany House, 2009).

35 Lloyd Cory, *Quote, Unquote* (Wheaton, Il: Victor Books, 1977), 197.

36 C. S. Lewis, *Mere Christianity*, rev. ed. (London: Fontana Books, 1955), 166.

37 Ibid., 114.

38 Abraham J. Heschel, *The Insecurity of Freedom* (New York: Schocken Books, 1972), 71–71, quoted in Houston and Parker, *A Vision for the Aging Church*, 55.

39 David Jeremiah, *Morning and Evening Devotions: Holy Moments in the Presence of God* (Nashville: Thomas Nelson, 2017), 699.

40 Douglas Beyer, "Our Father", Christians.org, 2001, http://www.christians.org/prayer/lordsprayer.htm.

41 Douglas Clark, quoted in Martin Wells Knapp, *Impressions* (McKinney, TX: Stover Creek, 2016), 50.

42 See Thomas Meyer, *The Memorization Study Bible: The New Testament* (Green Forest, AR: New Leaf Press, 2018).

43 "Does God Still Speak to Us?", Bible.org, 20 July 2009, https://bible.org/illustration/does-god-still-speak-us.

44 Samuel C. Williamson, *Hearing God in Conversation: How to Recognize His Voice Everywhere* (Grand Rapids: Kregel, 2016), 27.

45 Martin Wells Knapp, *Impressions*.

46 Roger Steer, *Hudson Taylor: Lessons in Discipleship* (Crowborough, UK: Monarch Books, 1995), 34.

47 Quoted in John MacNeil, *The Spirit-Filled Life* (Chicago: Bible Institute Colportage Association, 1895), chap. XII, http://www.gutenberg.org/cache/epub/33247/pg33247.html.

48 Jonathan Swift, *Gulliver's Travels* (1726), 14, https://www.planetebook.com/free-ebooks/gullivers-travels.pdf.

49 Adrian van Kaam and Susan Muto, *Aging Gracefully* (Boston: St. Paul's Books and Media, 1992), 13.

50 Paul Tournier, *Learn to Grow Old*, trans. Edwin Hudson (Louisville, KY: Westminster John Knox Press, 1972), 171.

51 Paul Tournier, *A Place For You: Psychology and Religion* (New York: Harper and Row, 1968), 164.

52 Margaret Magdalen, *A Spiritual Check-Up: Avoiding Mediocrity in the Christian Life* (Guildford: Highland, 1990).

53 Willard, *Renovation of the Heart*, 139.

54 R. A. Torrey's, "How to be inexpressibly happy" (sermon, Bethany Bible Church, 2003), http://www.bethanybible.org/archive/2003/030203.htm.

55 William Temple, quoted in Donald P. Hustad, *Jubilate! Church Music in the Evangelical Tradition* (Carol Stream, Il: Hope, 1981), 78.

56 William L. Kynes, "Charles Wesley", *Knowing and Doing*, Spring 2010, 2, http://www.cslewisinstitute.org/webfm_send/632.

57 M. Robert Mulholland Jr., *Invitation to a Journey: A Road Map for Spiritual Formation* (Downers Grove: Inter-Varsity Press, 1993), 101.

58 Frederick Buechner, *The Sacred Journey* (San Francisco: Harper and Row, 1982), 21–22.

59 Richard B. Hays and Judith C. Hays, "The Christian Practice of Growing Old: The Witness of Scripture", in Hauerwas et al., eds., *Growing Old in Christ*, 13.

60 Jean Vanier, *Becoming Human* (Mahwah, New Jersey: Paulist Press, 1998), 2.

61 John Calvin, *Institutes of the Christian Religion*, trans. Henry Beveridge (London, 1599), book 1, chap. 1, 1–2, https://reformed.org/books/institutes/books/book1/bk1ch01.html.

62 Richard Dawkins, *The Selfish Gene* (New York: Oxford University Press, 1976), 2.

63 Thomas Hobbes, *Leviathan* (London, 1651), Chapter XIII, "Of the Natural Condition of Mankind As Concerning Their Felicity, and Misery", http://www.gutenberg.org/files/3207/3207-h/3207-h.htm#link2HCH0013.

64 Henri Nouwen, *Reaching Out: The Three Movements of the Spiritual Life* (New York: Doubleday Image Books, 1986).

65 Augustine, *The Confessions*, trans. J. G. Pilkington, Nicene and Post-Nicene Fathers, 1st ser., vol. 1 (Buffalo, NY: Christian Literature, 1887), chap. 1, http://www.newadvent.org/fathers/110101.htm.

66 Kathleen Fischer, *Winter Grace: Spirituality and Aging* (Nashville: Upper Room Books, 1998), 32.

67 Stanley Hauerwas and Laura Yordy, "Captured in Time: Friendship and Aging", in Hauerwas et al., eds., *Growing Old in Christ*, 178.

68 Charles R. Swindoll, *Growing Strong in the Seasons of Life* (Portland, OR: Multnomah Press, 1983), 349.

69 "The Senility Prayer", Beliefnet, accessed 18 December 2018, http://www.beliefnet.com/inspiration/2001/01/senility-prayer.aspx.

70 See Maria Josephine McErlane, "Friendship according to Augustine", *Review for Religious* 41, no. 4 (July-August 1982): 596–604; St. Thomas Aquinas, trans. Thomas Gilby, *Theological Texts* (London: Oxford University Press, 1955) 208–211; Aelred of Rievaulx, *Spiritual Friendship*, ed. Marsha L. Dutton, trans. Lawrence C. Braceland, Cistercian Fathers Series, no. 5 (Kalamazoo: Cistercian, 1977); Francis de Sales, *Introduction to the Devout Life*, trans. John K. Ryan (New York: Harper and Row, 1966), pt. 3, chap. 17–22.

71 Aelred of Rievaulx, *Spiritual Friendship*, ed. Marsha L. Dutton, trans. Lawrence C. Braceland (Collegeville, MN: Liturgical Press, 2010) 112–113.

72 Paula Ripple, *Called to be Friends* (Notre Dame, IN: Ave Maria Press, 1980), chap. 6.

73 See Jernigan and Jernigan, *Aging in Chinese Society*, 103. One of the conclusions of the authors' study is that in the case of Chinese elders, "the family continues to be the primary source of meaning and purpose for life". This may also be said of other cultures, though social changes in family structures and attitudes may affect the role of the family in the life of seniors.

74 Jack O. Balswick and Judith K. Balswick, *The Family: A Christian Perspective on the Contemporary Home*, (Michigan: Baker Book House, 1989), 19–33.

75 See Robert M. Solomon, *Fire for the Journey: Reflections for a God-guided Life* (Singapore: Armour, 2002), 35.

76 See Robert M. Solomon, *Faithful to the End: A Preacher's Exposition of 2 Timothy* (Grand Rapids: Discovery House, 2014).

77 See for example Howard G. Hendricks and William D. Hendricks, *As Iron Sharpens Iron: Building Character in a Mentoring Relationship* (Chicago: Moody Publishers, 1999); Paul D. Stanley and J. Robert Clinton, *Connecting: The Mentoring Relationships You Need To Succeed In Life* (Colorado: NavPress, 1992).

78 Tournier, *Learn to Grow Old*, 19.

79 Hays and Hays, "The Christian Practice of Growing Old", 17.

80 Cf. King David who "died at a ripe old age, full of days, riches, and honor" (1 Chronicles 29:28, HCSB).

81 The significant difference between the two genders can be found in neuropsychiatrist Dr Louann Brizendine's *The Female Brain* (New York: Broadway Books, 2006). Others, such as psychologist Dr Matthias Mehl, have produced figures that are almost similar, about 15,700 words for men and 16,200 for women; see Julie Hyunh, "Study Finds No Difference in the Amount Men and Women Talk", 19 June 2014, University of Arizona Undergraduate Biology Research Program Gazette, https://ubrp.arizona.edu/study-finds-no-difference-in-the-amount-men-and-women-talk/.

82 *Vitae Patrum: Sayings of the Egyptian Fathers* (sixth century; Vitae Patrum, 2004), Appendix 3, http://www.vitae-patrum.org.uk/page161.html.

83 Lee Strobel, *The Case for Miracles* (Grand Rapids: Zondervan, 2018), 16–17.

84 See Robert M. Solomon, *The Trinity and the Christian Life: Sound Doctrine for Faithful Discipleship* (Singapore: Genesis Books, 2016), chapter 9.

85 See Robert E. Seymour, *Aging Without Apology: Living the Senior Years with Integrity and Faith* (Valley Forge, PA: Judson Press, 1995), chapter 6, "Avoiding an Obsession with Health".

86 Charles H. Spurgeon, *An All Round Ministry: Address to Ministers and Students* (Edinburgh: The Banner of Truth Trust, 1960), 126–127.

87 Helen Oppenheimer, "Reflections on the Experience of Aging", in *Aging*, eds. Lisa Sowle Cahill and Dietmar Mieth (Philadelphia, PA: Trinity Press, 1996), 41–44.

88 Rowan A. Greer, "Special Gift and Special Burden: Views of Old Age in the Early Church", in Hauerwas et al., eds., *Growing Old in Christ*, 19–37.

89 Clement of Alexandria, *The Instructor*, Ante-Nicene Fathers, vol. 2 (Buffalo: Christian Literature, 1885–1896), 3.3, cf. 3.11.

90 Bianchi, *Aging as a Spiritual Journey*, 15.

91 "Gov. Lamm asserts elderly, if very ill, have 'duty to die'", *New York Times*, 29 March 1984.

92 Salma Khalik, "Ageing Well and Staying Healthy", *Straits Times*, 21 October 2018.

93 A helpful book is Una Kroll, *Growing Older* (London: Fount Paperbacks, 1988). Kroll, a church deaconess and medical doctor, offers practical advice on the problems of aging and threats to health.

94 William Mountford, *Euthanasy or Happy Talk Towards the End of Life* (Cambridge: Metcalf, 1848), 3–4, quoted in Bianchi, *Aging as a Spiritual Journey*, 183.

95 T. S. Eliot, "East Coker", in *The Complete Poems and Plays of T. S. Eliot* (London: Faber, 1973), 183.

96 Fischer, *Winter Grace*, 2.

97 Eugene S. Geissler, *The Best is Yet To Be: Life's Meaning in the Aging Years* (Notre Dame, IN: Ave Maria Press, 1988), 47.

98 Kenneth W. Osbeck, *101 Hymn Stories: The Inspiring True Stories Behind 101 Favorite Hymns* (Grand Rapids: Kregel, 2012), 52.

99 C. H. Spurgeon, *Lectures to My Students: Being Addresses Delivered to the Students of the Pastors' College, Metropolitan Tabernacle* (New York: Robert Carter and Brothers, 1889) vol. 1, 167.

100 Archibald D. Hart, *Coping with Depression in the Ministry and Other Helping Professions* (Waco, TX: Word, 1984).

101 See David Martyn Lloyd-Jones, *Spiritual Depression: Its Causes and Its Cures* (Grand Rapids: William B. Eerdmans, 1965).

102 Michael Butler and Ann Orbach, *Being Your Age: Pastoral Care for Older People* (London: SPCK, 1993), 62–63.

103 Joan D. Chittister, *The Gift of Years: Growing Older Gracefully* (New York: Bluebridge, 2008), 221

104 Fischer, *Winter Grace*, 126.

105 See Kua Ee Heok, *Colours of Aging: 30 Years of Research on the Mental Health of the Singapore Elderly* (Singapore: Write Editions, 2017).

106 David Keck, *Forgetting Whose We Are: Alzheimer's Disease and the Love of God* (Nashville: Abingdon Press, 1996).

107 Ibid. chapter 8.

108 Lewis, *Mere Christianity*, 116.

109 See Nuccio Ordine, *The Usefulness of the Useless*, trans. Alastair McEwan (Philadelphia: Paul Dry Books, 2017). Ordine shows how utilitarianism has invaded culture, the academia, and the marketplace, with dire consequences for human dignity and society.

110 Thomas C. Oden, *The Structures of Awareness* (Nashville: Abingdon Press, 1969). See also Thomas C. Oden, *Two Worlds: Notes on the Death of Modernity in America & Russia* (Downers Grove: Inter-Varsity Press, 1992), 103–104.

111 J. I. Packer, *Rediscovering Holiness: Know the Fullness of Life with God* (Ventura, CA: Regal, 2009), 225–226.

112 Robert Browning, "Rabbi Ben Ezra", in *The Poetical Works of Robert Browning*, vol. 1 (London: Smith and Elder, 1899), 580.

113 Adam Clarke, "2 Timothy 4:22", in *Commentary on the Whole Bible* (1832), http://www.studylight.org/com/acc/view.cgi?bk=54&ch=4.

114 Joni Eareckson Tada, quoted in *Inspired Faith 365 Days a Year: Daily Motivation in God's Word* (Nashville: Thomas Nelson, 2012), 93.

115 Oswald Chambers, "11 February", in *My Utmost For His Highest* (Grand Rapids: Discovery House, 2017).

116 Bernard of Clairvaux, *On Loving God* (Pickerington, OH: Beloved, 2014), chap. 8–9.

117 Van Kaam and Muto, *Aging Gracefully*, 13.

118 H. Glen Lanier, "For All the Joys of Living", no. 4 in *10 New Hymns on Aging and the Later Years* (Fort Worth, TX: Hymn Society of America, 1976).

119 James Allen Francis, *One Solitary Life* (1963), 1–7. The original text was published as a pamphlet, and was published with some modifications in *The Irish Echo*, 27 December 1969.

120 Bianchi, *Aging as a Spiritual Journey*, 169.

121 Clarke, "Mark 9:49", https://www.studylight.org/commentaries/acc/mark-9.html.

122 Thomas à Kempis, *The Imitation of Christ*, ed. Harold C Gardiner (New York: Doubleday, 2009), 1:23, 1:33.

123 See William J. Carl Jr., ed., *Graying Gracefully: Preaching to Older Adults* (Louisville, KY: Westminster John Knox Press, 1997). The book is a collection of essays on the topic and model sermons.

124 J. I. Packer, *Finishing Our Course with Joy: Guidance from God for Engaging with Our Aging* (Wheaton: Crossway, 2014), 22.

125 Hammarskjöld, *Markings*, 89.

ABOUT THE PUBLISHER

Discovery House Publishing™ produces a wide array
of premium and quality resources that focus on Scripture,
show reverence for God and His Word, demonstrate
the relevance of vibrant faith, and equip and encourage you
to draw closer to God in all seasons of your life.

NOTE TO THE READER

We invite you to share your response to the
message in this book by writing to us at:
5 Pereira Road #07-01
Asiawide Industrial Building
Singapore 368025

or sending an email to:
dhpsingapore@dhp.org

Made in the USA
Coppell, TX
22 July 2022